EFFECTIVE BUSINESS MEETINGS

PREPARING FOR EFFECTIVE BUSINESS MEETINGS

Have you ever sat through a meeting that you felt was a waste of your time? Maybe the meeting wasn't relevant to you or it was just poorly run. Perhaps it lacked a clear purpose. The root cause of ineffective meetings is almost always poor planning.

Meetings are among the most expensive forms of communication in today's business environment, so it's essential to make the investment worthwhile. No matter their format, effective meetings efficiently meet their objectives and encourage an atmosphere of open participation that's characterized by fairness and order.

Effective meetings begin with careful preparation. This course outlines a five-step process for preparing for effective meetings. First, you'll learn how to clarify the purpose and objectives of a meeting. Second, you'll learn how to determine if the meeting is required, or if a meeting alternative can fulfill the objectives. Third, you'll learn how to choose the best participants. Fourth, you'll learn how to create the agenda. And fifth, you'll learn how to prepare yourself and your participants for a successful meeting.

The next time you need to prepare a meeting, the methods introduced in this course will help you make the most of you and your participants' valuable time. By making your meetings as effective as possible, you'll work to conserve company resources, establish a reputation as considerate and efficient, and attract greater contributions from your attendees.

THE VALUE OF PLANNING MEETINGS

The value of planning meetings
Ineffective and inefficient meetings are a waste of time for the people who have interrupted their busy schedules to attend them. As a result, these people can become frustrated and discouraged from becoming involved in future meetings.

A meeting takes place when a group gathers to address one or more tasks or issues.

Many meetings are often ineffective because leaders lack the skills and techniques required to make meetings more effective.

When meetings are ineffective, it's often because of an unclear purpose, or an ineffective agenda and facilitation strategies. Sometimes, meetings are too long or held too often, or the results aren't noted. These problems, and many others, can be addressed through good planning.

See each way in which meetings can be rendered ineffective to learn more about it.

Unclear purpose
Poorly planned meetings often lack a clear purpose. As a result, objectives aren't met and the organizer's credibility can be compromised.

Agenda or facilitation
Poor planning often yields agenda or facilitation strategies that fail to achieve the desired result. Without properly designed strategies, attendees can't prepare in advance and meetings can veer off topic.

Too long or too often
Meetings are an expensive form of communication, so arranging too many of them can be costly. Meetings that are too long are tiring, which can diminish their effectiveness, often compromising their outcome. This often reduces confidence in the project and its organizers.

Results aren't noted
Failing to record and communicate the outcome of a meeting can give employees the impression that the meeting was unnecessary, which can negatively affect attendance in the future.

Effective meetings must have a clear purpose and agenda so they can start and end on time. They require a structure to stay on track, and they should also provide clear follow-up action. Finally, meetings should encourage a variety of perspectives in order to generate positive ideas and solutions.

Making meetings as effective as possible is important for four reasons. The first is their high cost. Second, meetings directly impact the quality of decisions. The third reason relates to the degree of buy-in from participants. Fourth, the effectiveness of follow-through encourages future commitment.

See each aspect of the importance of effective meetings to learn more about it.

Cost
Meetings are one of the most expensive forms of workplace communication. The expense can be calculated by taking the number of attendees and determining the hourly value for each person's time. Next, multiply this figure by the number of hours the meeting is set to last, plus the number of hours needed for preparation time.

For example, a manager holds a meeting with five employees. The hourly cost for each employee is $35 per hour. If the meeting will last three hours, and requires three hours of preparation, the meeting will cost more than $1,000 for the five employees. Since the average employee attends at least seven meetings per week, it's crucial that meetings are as efficient as possible.

Quality of decisions

Decision-making is often stifled because either the right people or the right information are missing. Important information is often held by people in different parts of an organization. Having access to the right information from the right sources improves the quality of decisions.

Degree of buy-in

Employee buy-in and support for decisions is essential for the success of any initiative. When employees feel like they're being heard, their degree of buy-in increases. Meetings are a good place to encourage this sense of cooperation through participation. When a significant level of buy-in is achieved, a general consensus for decisions may be reached.

A cooperative meeting atmosphere is also an effective venue for resolving any conflicts that arise. Since ongoing conflicts can impede progress, it's especially important that time be devoted to conflict resolution.

Effectiveness of follow-through

Effective meetings encourage commitment and focus, and they create a clear sense of what needs to be accomplished. Since a meeting often ends with the distribution of assignments, individuals often feel empowered to achieve their tasks with a greater sense of vigor. For example, employees may become more knowledgeable about how their work fits into the organization as a whole.

Because meetings are costly, they must be as productive as possible. Productive meetings require thorough planning, which can be time consuming and labor intensive. But strong planning is one of the surest ways to maximize your investment.

However, there are several challenges to planning effective meetings. First, employees are increasingly busy. They're often out of the office, or in different locations. So organizing meetings at a time and place that suits everyone can be difficult.

The structure of organizations can also be a challenge when planning meetings. Today, organizations tend to grant more responsibility to employees and thus demand more participation from them at meetings. This can result in more perspectives vying for attention which can make keeping meetings on schedule more difficult.

Another challenge arises from employee turnover. Newer employees may need to be introduced to company protocols in meetings, which may frustrate existing employees already familiar with such details.

As the size of meetings increases, so should your planning efforts. Similarly, meetings addressing more complex issues will require more planning time to be successful.

For example, Kate manages the Accounting Department at a retail company. Recently, some changes to tax laws have arisen and Kate has called a meeting to discuss them. As part of her planning, Kate has invited only one accountant from each department.

As a result, Kate receives valuable information from each department at a relatively low cost. Attendees are satisfied because they've had the opportunity to contribute ideas to new policies, and they're pleased to attend future meetings with Kate.

Question

Sandra has decided that she needs to call a meeting to address a budgetary issue with her team.

What examples reflect positive outcomes associated with her carefully planning the meeting?

Options:
1. She determines how much time the meeting requires, minimizing expense
2. She invites people who are directly related to the issue, encouraging the best possible decision
3. She anticipates objections to her solution and prepares counterarguments to ensure consensus
4. She examines each task that she plans to assign so individuals won't ask questions later
5. She explains how the tasks she's assigned fit into the

team's goal, instilling a sense of vigor in its members
6. She makes sure employees can speak in the meeting and support the decision, even if it isn't their preference

Answer

Option 1: *This option is correct. Meetings are among the most expensive forms of communication in offices, so they should be carefully planned so as to make the investment worthwhile.*

Option 2: *This option is correct. Good decisions are a result of careful planning. By gathering the right people, along with the right information, the quality of decisions is enhanced.*

Option 3: *This option is incorrect. Good planning should encourage an open exchange of diverse ideas to reach effective solutions that have wide appeal, not to promote one's personal agenda.*

Option 4: *This option is incorrect. A well-planned meeting often makes employees eager to complete their tasks. However, an effectively run meeting should also provide them with a better idea of who they can speak with about specific aspects of it.*

Option 5: *This option is correct. People often feel energized after an effective meeting, and, after seeing how their roles fit into the organization, they may take initiative when completing their next tasks.*

Option 6: *This option is correct. When employees feel like they've made a contribution, they tend to form a consensus more easily because they feel as though their voices have been heard.*

Summary

Ineffective meetings are all too common in organizations today and most often occur because of poor planning.

Planning effective meetings has four general benefits. First, meetings are an expensive form of communication, and making them as efficient as possible is essential for keeping costs down. Second, effective meetings tend to yield good decision-making. Third, when participants are able to voice their perspectives, it increases their level of buy-in, which means they'll likely support initiatives more readily. Finally, distributing assignments at the end of meetings keeps the attendees involved and eager to achieve their tasks. This also encourages them to participate in future meetings.

DETERMINING MEETING PURPOSE, OBJECTIVES, AND NECESSITY

Determining purpose and objectives

Effective meetings are the result of careful preparation. Simply assuming that things will work out can lead to a poorly run meeting that frustrates people. To help you prepare an effective meeting, there are five steps you can follow. First, determine the purpose and objectives of the meeting. Second, determine if the meeting is necessary. Third, choose participants. Fourth, create the agenda. And fifth, prepare yourself and others.

You need to identify what you want to achieve, and then determine if a meeting is the best way to do it. For this reason, the first step of planning a successful meeting is to determine the purpose and objectives of the meeting. Carefully setting the objectives of the meeting will give it purpose and direction.

First, you should consider which type of meeting will best suit your needs. One example is a workshop that features a group of tasks intended to guide the participation of attendees in order to achieve a given goal.

Another example is a working session. Here, participants team up to complete a particular task.

A final example is an informational meeting, where the goal is simply to share information gathered by the group's members or their departments.

Effective meetings have a clear purpose and set of objectives. These need to be carefully considered as part of the first step in preparing for an effective meeting.

See each aspect of a meeting to learn more about it.

Purpose

A meeting's purpose – or high-level-goal – can be determined by asking simple questions such as "Why are we having the meeting?" "What are we trying to accomplish?" and "Who are we reporting to?"

For example, the purpose of a meeting could be to exchange information, build support for a new initiative, or teach new skills.

Objectives

Meeting objectives are the more specific aims that describe how a meeting's purpose will be

accomplished. For objectives to be effective, they must be results-oriented and measurable.

There are two questions you can ask to help determine your objectives. First, "How will the goal or purpose be achieved?" And second, "How will meeting success be measured?"

Consider Peter, a project manager for a marketing company. He's planning a meeting with his team regarding a new campaign. The purpose of the meeting is to generate and develop new themes for the campaign.

Peter decides that he'll hold a brainstorming session to begin the meeting. Initially he thinks he'll set "choose the best ideas from the session" as the meeting's objective. However, he then realizes this objective is neither measurable nor results-oriented, and so it isn't appropriate.

He reconsiders and determines that "decide on the best idea by popular vote" is a much stronger objective. This is because it contributes directly to the meeting's purpose, is results-oriented, and is measurable – that is, it can be easily recognized as achieved or not.

Question
Classify each example as a meeting purpose, an effective objective, or an ineffective objective. Each classification may apply to more than one example.

Options:

A. Purpose

B. Effective objective C. Ineffective objective

Targets:
1. Generate ideas to circumvent budget constraints
2. Find ways to reduce spending by at least 13%
3. Discuss ways to reduce wasted resources
4. Review individual and team responsibilities
5. Provide each team with an overview of its responsibilities and have all members report on their roles
6. Discuss the roles of teams and their members and how they interact with each other

Answer

*This is an example of a meeting's purpose, which is a high-level goal of what the meeting
should achieve.*

This is an example of an effective objective because it describes how to achieve a goal in a measurable and results-oriented way.

This is an example of an ineffective objective because while it describes how the goal may be achieved and is results-oriented to a degree, it isn't measurable. It will therefore be difficult to judge whether the meeting was successful.

This is an example of a meeting's purpose because it's a high-level goal that will be made more specific in well-stated objectives.

This is an example of an effective objective because it is, above all, results-oriented and easily understood as achieved or not.

This is an example of an ineffective objective because it doesn't offer concrete criteria for measuring success or failure. In this way, it won't provide a solid structure for a meeting.

Determining meeting timing

The second step for preparing for an effective business meeting is to determine whether or not a meeting is required. Because employees are busy and meetings can be costly, you should call a meeting only when the time is right and cheaper alternatives have been rejected, or when secondary reasons make a meeting feasible.

To decide whether a meeting is required, you can ask yourself three questions. First, "Is this the right time to have a meeting?" Second, "Will a meeting alternative fulfill the purpose?" And third, "Are there other reasons to hold the meeting?" These three questions form a decision tree that you can use to help you decide if a meeting is the best choice.

The decision tree represents the three questions for determining the necessity of a meeting. If the first question, "Is this the right time for a meeting?" is answered with no, the result is "Postpone or add to the agenda of another meeting." If the answer is yes, the next question is "Will a meeting alternative fulfill the purpose?" If no, the result is "Plan a meeting." If the answer is yes, the next question of the decision tree is "Are there other reasons to hold the meeting?" If the answer is yes, the conclusion is to "Plan a meeting;" if the answer is no, the conclusion is to "Choose a meeting alternative."

There are three things to consider when asking the first question, "Is this the right time to have a meeting?" First, will you have sufficient information available at the time of the meeting to present, consider, and decide on a course of action? If not, the meeting should be postponed until this information becomes available.

Second, can the meeting wait until another time? If so, it may be useful to add the issue to the agenda of another meeting, unless it requires its own meeting.

Finally, are the purpose and objectives of the meeting clear? If you haven't been able to come up with a clear purpose or objective, that usually means you don't need a meeting.

For example, Megan is a business leader with a renewable energy company. She wants to call a meeting to discuss a venture the company has asked her department to consider.

Megan has been given a report on the company's research into the viability of the project, and one of the report's authors will be in the office next week. Megan has also decided that the issue is complex enough to warrant its own meeting.

Finally, Megan has already determined that the purpose of the meeting will be to decide whether her team has the time and resources to take on the project. Having her team members report on their availability and comfort with the tasks is one of the meeting's objectives. The other is to conduct a popular vote as to whether they should accept the project.

Question

What things should you consider when deciding whether the time is right for a meeting?

Options:

1. Whether enough information will be available to address the issue
2. Whether it can wait until a later time
3. Whether the meeting's purpose and objectives are clear
4. Whether everyone you plan to invite is available
5. Whether other meetings are scheduled for the same time

Answer

Option 1: This option is correct. A meeting should only be called when the necessary information will be available.

Option 2: This option is correct. If an issue isn't urgent, it may be postponed or added to another meeting's agenda.

Option 3: This option is correct. If the objectives or purpose aren't clear, the meeting likely isn't necessary.

Option 4: This option is incorrect. A meeting's necessity relates to information, its purpose and objectives rather than the list of attendees.

Option 5: This option is incorrect. At this stage, you need to have the right information available, a sense of urgency, and a clear purpose and set of objectives, instead of scheduling conflicts that might arise.

Determining alternatives

When deciding whether a meeting is necessary, the second ques-

tion you should ask is, "Will a meeting alternative fulfill the purpose?" In addition to being costly, a meeting may not be the only – or the most effective – method of achieving your objectives. Different forms of communication can be considered if your meeting purpose includes information sharing and building awareness, generating ideas, solving problems, and gaining new skills or knowledge.
See each meeting purpose to learn about meeting alternatives.

Information sharing and building awareness
E-mails and memos may be more direct methods of communication to inform others. These methods are much less expensive ways to share information and can often achieve the same objectives as a meeting.

Generating ideas
Meetings are often called to brainstorm ideas or solutions. However, you can obtain a similar variety of responses by circulating surveys or worksheets electronically. Anonymous brainstorming may also encourage individuals who are reluctant to speak in groups to suggest their own creative ideas.

Solving problems
By circulating a survey to the appropriate individuals, you can generate a variety of solutions to a problem. Once several viable options have been selected, you can vote to find out which solution is most popular.

Gaining new skills or knowledge
Training sessions can be an expensive type of meeting and can leave those unable to attend behind the rest of the group. E-learning or remote training sessions are valuable alternatives that offer greater flexibility than in-office sessions. Independent practice following training can be useful to encourage the development of new skills in a private environment.

Although there are many alternatives to meetings, some tasks are best dealt with in a meeting. Production-related tasks, hands-on training, and team-building exercises all rely on face-to-face interaction or the use of onsite materials. Meetings are especially beneficial when collaboration or idea-sharing is required, particularly when various perspectives need to be expressed.

Question

What examples describe situations where a meeting isn't necessary?

Options:
1. The criteria for decision-making on the key issue are under review and won't be finalized in time for the proposed meeting
2. The issue can be added to the agenda of a meeting already planned for two weeks from now
3. The meeting leader is clear on what should be accomplished at the meeting
4. The purpose of the meeting is to circulate the results of the latest marketing campaign to familiarize department heads with the numbers
5. The purpose of the meeting is to elicit a number of perspectives on the new marketing campaign

Answer

Option 1: This option is correct. If sufficient information won't be available to consider at the time of the meeting, the meeting should be delayed until the information is available.

Option 2: This option is correct. If an issue is simple to address and fits in with the theme of an already planned meeting, it's often wise to simply add it to that meeting's agenda.

Option 3: This option is incorrect. Being clear on what the meeting intends to accomplish is actually a reason to hold a meeting.

Option 4: This option is correct. Many meeting objectives can be met through alternative methods of communication. In this case, circulating the material via e-mail is more direct and cheaper.

Option 5: This option is incorrect. This option describes a reason that may in fact warrant a meeting, the presence of a variety of perspectives in one place.

Identifying other reasons

The third question to ask when determining whether a meeting is required is, "Are there other reasons to hold the meeting?" There can be benefits associated with holding a meeting that reach beyond the specific issue at hand.

For example, Martin is a branch manager at a bank. He considered calling a meeting to discuss some changes the bank had implemented regarding the issuing of small business loans.

Martin thought that this information could simply be distributed to his loans team by e-mail, since it didn't require a lot of interaction or sharing of perspectives.

However, he also recognized that it had been some time since the team had a chance to engage in team-building. With this secondary benefit in mind, Martin called the meeting after all so that he could discuss the changes with his team, while also using the opportunity to strengthen the team's bond.

Another secondary advantage of holding a meeting is when you want to have a variety of perspectives in one place. The atmosphere created by having several different perspectives gathered together can be useful for generating creative solutions or ideas, and can be hard to replicate through meeting alternatives.

For example, the regional manager of a retail chain is debating whether to call a meeting with a large group of store managers to address a growing list of customer complaints. It will be costly to gather all of the managers together. However, the extent of the group's knowledge relating to customer complaints outweighs the cost.

Since the variety of opinions will greatly improve the company's chance of addressing the right issues and improving its reputation, the meeting becomes a worthwhile investment.

Finally, if a meeting is required but isn't feasible, you may consider holding a virtual meeting. Virtual meetings use different kinds of technology to connect individuals in different locations and allow them to participate as if they were in a room together.

Virtual meetings include conference calls, video conferencing, and web conferencing.

The advantages of virtual meetings include reduced costs, reduced interruption to participants' schedules, and greater task focus. This is because people tend to be less distracted by things like emotion when they aren't in the presence of other people.

Virtual meetings also have a number of disadvantages. Gaps in communication can lead to confusion and delays. Virtual meetings typically run at a slower pace, and participants may encounter logistical problems related to voting, discussion activities, security, and confidentiality.

Case Study: Question 1 of 2

Scenario

For your convenience, the case study is repeated with each question.

You're a manager at an engineering firm that has recently been bought by a large multinational organization. This change in ownership will undoubtedly affect the employees, but you believe that the changes will be almost entirely positive. Nevertheless, many employees are concerned that their previous autonomy may be compromised, while others fear their jobs may be in jeopardy.

You're trying to determine whether you should call a meeting to detail the changes and how they're likely to impact employees. You could give a presentation and have a structured question and answer period, or you could e-mail your employees the details of the changes and invite them to respond with questions or concerns. However, when considering the number of employees that would need to attend the meeting and the time it would take to relay all the information, holding a meeting would be expensive. Cost is a particular concern because the acquiring company is looking for places to improve cost efficiency.

Answer the questions in order to determine whether or not you should hold a meeting in this case.

Question

Given the circumstances, should you plan a meeting to discuss the changes?

The flowchart represents the three questions for determining the necessity of a meeting. If the first question, "Is this the right time for a meeting?" is answered with no, the result is "Postpone or add to the agenda of another meeting." If the answer is yes, the next question is "Will a meeting alternative fulfill the purpose?" If no, the result is "Plan a meeting." If the answer is yes, the next question of the chart is "Are there other reasons to hold the meeting?" If the answer is yes, the conclusion is to "Plan a meeting;" if the answer is no, the conclusion is to "Choose a meeting alternative."

Options:
1. Yes, a meeting is the right option in this case
2. A meeting isn't the right option at the moment

Answer

Option 1: *This is the correct option. A meeting is warranted in this case and will likely be worth the time and expense.*

Option 2: *This option is incorrect. There are a number of circumstances in this case that collectively justify holding a meeting.*

Case Study: Question 2 of 2

Scenario

For your convenience, the case study is repeated with each question.

You're a manager at an engineering firm that has recently been bought by a large multinational organization. This change in ownership will undoubtedly affect the employees, but you believe that the changes will be almost entirely positive. Nevertheless, many employees are concerned that their previous autonomy may be compromised, while others fear their jobs may be in jeopardy.

You're trying to determine whether you should call a meeting to detail the changes and how they're likely to impact employees. You could give a presentation and have a structured question and answer period, or you could e-mail your employees the details of the changes and invite them to respond with questions or concerns. However, when considering the number of employees that would need to attend the meeting and the time it would take to relay all the information, holding a meeting would be expensive. Cost is a particular concern because the acquiring company is looking for places to improve cost efficiency.

Answer the questions in order to determine whether or not you should hold a meeting in this case.

Question

Why did you decide for or against calling a meeting?

Options:
1. The meeting's purpose and objectives are clear
2. The secondary advantage of engaging those who may be concerned about the changes makes the meeting worthwhile
3. Sending an e-mail that details the changes and their impact to each employee will sufficiently fulfill each of the meeting's objectives
4. There isn't sufficient information available
5. The meeting's objectives can easily be added to the agenda of another meeting that's already planned

Answer

Option 1: This option is correct. The meeting is appropriate since it is needed to raise awareness and build support for the upcoming changes.

Option 2: This option is correct. If the meeting's sole objective is to raise awareness about the changes, an e-mail could be a viable alternative. However, since it is also intended to build support, a meeting is warranted.

Option 3: This option is incorrect. While an e-mail will raise awareness about the breadth of changes, it isn't able to build support for the changes in the same way that a meeting can.

Option 4: This option is incorrect. The purpose of the meeting is to discuss the changes and how they'll impact individuals, so the information has to do with how the acquiring company differs from the current one. This information is already known before the meeting will take place.

Option 5: This option is incorrect. A meeting of this magnitude, that would require this many participants, isn't appropriate as an addition to another meeting's agenda.

Summary

The first step of planning an effective meeting is to determine the meeting's purpose and objectives.

The second step is to determine if a meeting is necessary. This can be done by asking whether this is the right time for a meeting, whether a meeting alternative can fulfill the purpose, and whether there are other reasons to hold the meeting.

SELECTING PARTICIPANTS AND CREATING THE MEETING AGENDA

Choosing participants

The first two steps in preparing for effective meetings are to determine your purpose and objectives, and then decide whether a meeting is really necessary. Now it's time for the third step, which is to choose the participants. In some cases, this may be quite clear. For example, a staff meeting will typically involve all the employees in a given department or office.

Graphic
The five steps to prepare for effective meetings are to determine purpose and objectives, determine if meeting is necessary, choose participants, create an agenda, and prepare yourself and others.

It might be more difficult, however, to decide who should participate in other types of meetings. For example, crossfunctional or problem-solving meetings typically invite participants who represent a department, or who have specialized knowledge of a certain area. Participants for such meetings are often selected for their particular skill sets.

So, who should you invite to your meeting? You want people who are able, and authorized, to represent their areas, organizations, or departments, and who are able to speak about them. This likely includes the managers of groups or projects that are directly involved in the issue your meeting is addressing.

You should also make sure that all stakeholders who will be affected by the outcome of your meeting are present. Also, try to have decision-makers present.

Finally, you should also include technical experts or advisors on key issues in your attendee list. These include individuals who are familiar with the product, process, or issue at hand.

Though you want the right people at your meeting, you also don't want too many participants. Too many attendees can make decision-making and discussion cumbersome.

Thus, people who can be informed via a follow-up e-mail or report likely don't need to attend the meeting. For example, people whose presence isn't essential or whose contributions are likely to be minimal can usually just be followed up with after the meeting.

And finally, depending on the purpose of the meeting and the sensitivity of the issue being addressed, the attendance of authority figures may not be appropriate. This is because their presence could inhibit others or stifle otherwise productive discussion.

Consider Mathilde, who is a manager at an advertising agency. She's planning a meeting to discuss how to attract a more diverse set of clients. First, she invites representatives from the print and online magazine, television, and radio divisions to speak about their current and desirable clients.

Mathilde also invites the agency's managing director, who wants to hear some of the new ideas before giving his approval. Mathilde, the managing director, and the representatives from each department are the decision-makers and stakeholders for this meeting.

However, she doesn't invite the advertising writers and photographers, or others who may be interested in the meeting but won't contribute to the meeting's purpose. Instead, she decides they can be kept informed of any decisions in an e-mail following the meeting.

Question
Who should be invited to a meeting?
Options:
1. Individuals who will be impacted by the meeting's outcome
2. Those who are interested in the meeting's outcome
3. Individuals who are involved in making a decision on something addressed in the meeting
4. Employees who are likely to benefit from observing the dynamics of a meeting setting
5. Capable and authorized representatives of a particular area covered in the meeting
6. Advisors on technical matters or key issues

Answer

Option 1: *This option is correct. People affected by the meeting should be present at the meeting.*

Option 2: *This option is incorrect. Too many attendees a meeting can impede its effectiveness, so interest may not warrant attendance.*

Option 3: *This option is correct. Key decision-makers should be present in meetings requiring their involvement.*

Option 4: *This option is incorrect. Attendees should be limited to those directly involved in the meeting.*

Option 5: *This option is correct. Having managers present will ensure you have the right information in your meeting.*

Option 6: *This option is correct. It's important to have someone who can explain the nature of an issue to the group present.*

Role of the agenda

The fourth step of your preparation for an effective meeting is to create the agenda. A meeting agenda is a list of tasks that's intended to achieve the meeting's objectives. In addition to the set of tasks, an agenda typically contains the meeting's topics, speakers, and schedule. The agenda for a meeting is usually made available to participants in advance.

There are two reasons to invest time in planning a meeting

agenda.

First, attendees can access the agenda before the meeting and conduct research to prepare for the meeting in advance. In this way, it helps to ensure quality participation – by helping attendees prepare good questions, for example.

A clear agenda also keeps the meeting on track and helps to avoid digressions into irrelevant topics.

Effective and ineffective agendas are characterized by whether they are realistic, are logical in their sequencing, have a clear purpose and objectives, and include only relevant items.

See each characteristic of agendas to learn more about it.

Realistic
Effective agendas are realistic about what can be sufficiently covered, and they allot enough time for each item. Ineffective agendas often include too many items and underestimate how much time is needed.

Logical
Effective agendas logically sequence items so that each leads up to the meeting's ultimate
purpose. An ineffective agenda usually fails to clarify the priority of items, which may result in some items being neglected.

Purpose and objectives
Effective agendas have both a clear purpose and objectives. Without them, an ineffective agenda fails to guide the meeting along.

Relevant items
An effective agenda includes only items that contribute to its purpose. An ineffective agenda may include items that distract from the purpose.

Question
What should an effective meeting agenda do?
Options:
1. Enable a meeting to achieve its purpose
2. Enable participants to prepare in advance
3. Ensure the meeting stays on track

4. Ensure that all the participants attend
5. Ensure you're aware who will and will not attend

Answer

Option 1: *This option is correct. An effective agenda is guided by the meeting's purpose and so works to achieve it.*

Option 2: *This option is correct. Having access to the meeting's agenda allows participants to do research and prepare questions.*

Option 3: *This option is correct. By adhering to a meeting agenda, issues that divert the meeting from the purpose are kept to a minimum.*

Option 4: *This option is incorrect. An agenda guides the meeting itself and helps attendees prepare, but it doesn't compel them to attend.*

Option 5: *This option is incorrect. The meeting's participant's should already be chosen by the time you create the agenda.*

Selecting agenda items

There are five steps you can follow to create an effective meeting agenda. First, establish the meeting's length. Second, list the agenda items that need to be covered. Third, screen and prioritize the items. Fourth, estimate the length of items. And fifth, schedule the items.

For example, Jessica is a manager at an online retail company. She's planning a meeting to discuss some changes to the online ordering and billing processes. To address the changes, the reasons for them, and their intended effects, Jessica has set aside a block of one-and-a-half hours for the meeting. She expects to spend an hour on the first item, and fifteen minutes on each of the next two, including discussion.

Once you've established the length of the meeting, the second step is to list the agenda items that need to be covered, or the steps that need to occur.

The central purpose of Jessica's meeting is to inform her team about the changes. Because the agenda items need to contribute to this purpose, she divides the purpose into its components. Thus, introducing the process changes, explaining the reasons for the changes, and discussing their intended effects are listed as the meeting items. Time permitting, Jessica also hopes to address any questions and concerns the employees may have.

Finally, Jessica also wants to use the meeting as an opportunity to discuss the distribution of two new brands.

The third step for creating an effective agenda is to screen and prioritize items. Criteria can be applied to determine if a certain item should be included as part of the agenda, and if so, what priority it should be given.

To do this, you should ask questions about any proposed items. For example, does the item fit with the purpose or objectives of the meeting? Is there a real need to address the item?

After you've screened the items, you should have a better idea of the scope of the meeting. The next step involves choosing one of a variety of options.

Question

Suppose you've created a list of potential agenda items for your meeting.

See whether you can correctly match each level of urgency to the appropriate action.

Options:

A. Related to the meeting purpose and urgently requiring attention

B. Related to the meeting purpose, but not urgent

C. Related to the meeting purpose, but doesn't require input of the whole team

D. Unrelated to the meeting purpose

Targets:

1. Include on the agenda
2. Consider postponing for another meeting
3. Consider delegating to a person or committee
4. Consider excluding

Answer

Items that are directly related to the meeting's purpose and objectives and require immediate attention should be included on the agenda.

Items that are relevant but aren't urgent issues may be postponed to another meeting if the agenda is already sufficiently lengthy.

If an issue won't benefit from the input of the whole team, it may be more effective to delegate it to an individual or another committee. Items unrelated to the meeting's purpose or objective are often best addressed in another meeting or context.

When Jessica screens and prioritizes her agenda items, she realizes that some tasks aren't as well suited to the meeting's purpose as others.

Introducing the process changes, the reasons for them, and their intended benefits are the main points of the meeting. Because these items are urgent, they're included on the agenda. Jessica removes the discussion about distributing new brands from the agenda because it doesn't relate to the meeting's main purpose.

Finally, to field questions and concerns from her employees, Jessica invites them to contact her by e-mail so that issues can be addressed more fully than in the meeting. Even though concerns relate to the purpose of the meeting, e-mail is a more effective way to address them.

Allocating time for agenda items

The next step in planning an effective meeting agenda is to estimate the length of items in the agenda. This step should include factoring in time for any dialogue that's expected.

You should consider a number of factors when creating your meeting agenda:

more participants typically require more time, since discussions take longer

if information sharing or expert presentations are required, allocate more time to bring participants up to speed, and

controversial or complex issues require more time for discussion

To help you to accurately estimate the time required, it's helpful to think of meetings as having of two basic components: meeting tasks and meeting processes.

See each meeting component to learn more about it.

Meeting tasks

Meeting tasks are the things you want to accomplish by the end of the meeting. These tasks can also include gathering employee opinions about changes, decisions, or proposals.

Meeting processes

Meeting processes, or facilitation techniques, are the ways in which the meeting tasks are accomplished. These include brainstorming sessions for generating ideas, votes for making decisions, and discussions for reaching consensus.

An in-depth discussion of facilitation techniques and processes is beyond the scope of this course. However, selecting the appropriate process for considering issues and the associated facilitation technique is essential to a meeting's success. This takes time, so you need to know which techniques and processes – if any – you'll use before allocating time to your agenda items.

As the meeting leader, you can keep track of meeting tasks and processes using a facilitator agenda. This is an expanded version of the meeting agenda that includes the meeting processes you've chosen for each agenda item, the facilitation techniques, and any supporting materials required.

When allocating time for each agenda item, remember to include some extra time at the end of each item. This time should be used to answer questions, defend rationales, and summarize important decisions. Finally, this added time allows you to transition more easily into your next item.

With her meeting items screened and prioritized, Jessica's next task is to estimate how much time to allot to each.

Introducing the process changes is paramount and will feature three different speakers. Jessica allows fifteen minutes for each speaker, plus an additional fifteen minutes for questions and comments. As such, this item is given a full hour.

Next, Jessica will speak about why the changes are being made, and allows herself fifteen minutes to cover this. Finally, the managing director will speak about the advantages he expects these changes to bring. He's also given fifteen minutes. This brings the meeting to the expected one-and-a-half hour total.

The fifth and final step for creating an effective agenda is to schedule the items. There are several things you should consider:

Aim to sequence items logically and in a way that leads up to your ultimate goal. For example, if one decision needs to be made before another can be considered, be sure to schedule it first.

Try to schedule any creative tasks earlier in the meeting, when people are fresh and more engaged.

Aim to cover routine items – such as the minutes of the last meeting – first.

Try to vary the intensity of topics, mixing lighter topics with more substantive ones that require a greater level of attention, to allow attendees a chance to regroup.

Try to include some extra time in case you've underestimated any items, or in case new issues arise and require attention.

To finish creating her agenda, Jessica schedules its items. She decides that she'll speak about the reasons for the changes first, and then have the managing director address the expected effects.

Only then will she move to introducing the process changes themselves, since this is the ultimate goal of the meeting. This will be the best time to have the meeting's participants ask questions about the changes.

In this way, Jessica has logically sequenced the meeting items. Each item now builds toward the final purpose of the meeting.

Question

Which recommendations should be taken into consideration as part of creating an effective agenda?

Options:
1. Consider that things like the number of participants or complex subjects may require extra time
2. Aim to cover tasks that require participants to be creative while they're still energized
3. Attend to routine items last, covering the key items first
4. Try to alternate between mentally taxing tasks and ones that are relatively simple

5. Attempt to leave some time at the end of the meeting
6. Allocate extra time for routine items such as reviewing the minutes of a previous meeting

Answer

Option 1: *This option is correct. Accurate estimations of time are a central feature of an effective meeting agenda, so recognizing the things that often require more time is key.*

Option 2: *This option is correct. An effective agenda will maximize the time you've allotted. Part of this includes ensuring that attendees can contribute in an effective manner.*

Option 3: *This option is incorrect. Routine items can be mundane and so should be covered before the more important or challenging issues are addressed.*

Option 4: *This option is correct. It can be taxing on meeting attendees to tackle one challenging issue after another, so aim to give them time to refresh by interspersing more demanding tasks with simpler ones.*

Option 5: *This option is correct. Questions are likely to arise over what's been covered, so having extra time to clarify and recap what's been discussed can be useful.*

Option 6: *This option is incorrect. The time required to cover routine items should be easily estimated and adhered to.*

A sample agenda lists the location of the meeting as Meeting room A, the date of the meeting as September 27th, the leader as Jessica Smith, and the time of the meeting being 10:00 until 11:30. It then lists the items to be covered. First, reasons for the changes which will be presented by Jessica and run form 10:00 until 10:15. Second, intended benefits will be presented by a representative from management, and run from 10:15 until 10:30. And third, the changes will be introduced. This will run from 10:30: until 11:30 and will begin with a customer service perspective from 10:30 until 10:45, followed by a web-design perspective from 10:45 until 11:00, then a supplier liasion perspective from 11:00 until 11:45 and will end with time for questions and summary comments, from 11:15 until 11:30.

Question

Sequence the examples of the steps for creating an effective agenda.

Options:
1. Warren decides that the meeting will last one hour
2. Warren lists the things he wants to cover in the meeting
3. Warren decides that he can cover one item at a later meeting
4. Warren assigns extra time for the discussion point he knows will be the most contentious
5. Warren plans to have a brainstorming session early in the meeting

Answer

Correct answer(s):

Warren decides that the meeting will last one hour is ranked. The first step for creating an effective agenda is establishing how long the meeting will last.

Warren lists the things he wants to cover in the meeting is ranked. The second step for creating an effective agenda is listing what you want to cover.

Warren decides that he can cover one item at a later meeting is ranked. The third step for creating an effective agenda is screening and prioritizing agenda items.

Warren assigns extra time for the discussion point he knows will be the most contentious is ranked. The fourth step for creating an effective agenda is estimating the length of time for each item.

Warren plans to have a brainstorming session early in the meeting is ranked. The fifth step for creating an effective agenda is scheduling items.

Finally, it's important that you ask your meeting's participants for feedback on the draft of the agenda you send out. This way you can solicit any ideas they might have about other things the agenda should cover.

Be sure to submit any suggestions you receive to the same screening, prioritization, and allocation process you used for the other items.

Question

Dolores is preparing a meeting agenda. She begins by deciding how much time she should allow for the meeting. Next, she lists the things that she needs to address in the meeting.

What should Dolores do next, as the third step of planning an effective meeting agenda?

Options:
1. Screen out items that are nonurgent, don't require the input of the whole team, or are unrelated to the purpose of the meeting
2. Prioritize routine items and screen out those unrelated to the purpose
3. Arrange items so that simple tasks are mixed in with complicated tasks
4. Allocate extra time for asking questions and achieving consensus on the solution

Answer

Option 1: *This is the correct option. The third step of preparing an effective agenda is to screen and prioritize the items, postponing, delegating, or omitting anything nonurgent or unrelated to the meeting's purpose or objectives.*

Option 2: *This option is incorrect. While the third step involves prioritizing items and screening out those unrelated to the purpose, routine items shouldn't be given priority. Rather, routine items should be covered quickly before the more important issues are addressed.*

Option 3: *This option is incorrect. The third step is to screen and prioritize the agenda items. This option describes the final step, where the items are scheduled.*

Option 4: *This option is incorrect. The third step is to screen and prioritize the meeting items. This option describes the fourth step, which is to estimate how long each item will take.*

Summary

The third step of preparing for an effective meeting is to select your participants. You should invite those who can speak on behalf of a department, project, or area. Stakeholders and decision-makers should also be present. Finally, experts or advisors on key issues should also be invited. Since having too many attendees present might be counterproductive, avoid inviting those whose contributions are likely to be minimal, or anyone who can followed up with afterward.

The fourth step is to create a meeting agenda. To do this you should first establish how long the meeting will last, list the items that need to be covered, and then screen and prioritize them. Then estimate how long each item will take, before scheduling the items according to their relevance to the meeting's goal.

PREPARING YOURSELF AND OTHERS FOR THE MEETING

Prepare yourself
Once you've determined the purpose of your meeting, checked that a meeting is the best way to achieve that purpose, chosen your participants, and created an agenda, the fifth and final step in preparing an effective meeting is to prepare yourself and others for the meeting. You can prepare yourself by checking the venue, equipment, and materials.
See each meeting component to learn more about it.

Venue
First, make sure you confirm the availability of the venue you plan to use. Also, make sure there isn't anything in or near the venue that could be a distraction.
Double-check that there are enough chairs for everyone and that each place affords a good view of any speakers or visual materials.
Equipment
Preparing the equipment that you plan to use in the meeting helps prevent disruptions. For example, realizing that the bulb in the projector is burned out when you begin a presentation can be frustrating for participants. Make sure that you've also confirmed the availability of the equipment, and that you know how to use it.
Check that the power outlets in the room work, and that you can get online if necessary. Do a test run with all the equipment you

plan to use before the meeting takes place.
Materials
Gather together all the materials you plan to present or circulate during the meeting. This might include relevant documents, reports, or handouts.

You may also want to check that your overheads or multimedia presentations are accurate and ready for use.

You also need to consider how the dynamics of the group may affect the meeting. Some factors that can influence group dynamics are how well the participants know each other and what their comfort levels are in meetings. This may depend on what relationships they have within the workplace – managers and reports, for instance. How attendees feel about issues meant to be covered in the meeting can also contribute to the group's dynamic.

How participants interact with you and with each other can depend on their shared knowledge and work habits. Being aware of these factors and the impact they can have on how meetings run can help you anticipate issues, and steer the group in a positive direction. This all results in a smoother, and ultimately more effective, meeting.

Consider Alan, who is holding a meeting for several coworkers and managers to discuss a new marketing campaign. In preparation, he visits the room he's booked to make sure that it's quiet and that there are enough chairs. He also checks that his presentation runs on the room's computer. Finally, Alan schedules a brainstorming session with several people before the managers that he's also invited arrive. Alan hopes that this will help some people contribute more freely, and maximize their time together.

Question
Mei is scheduled to run a meeting tomorrow.
What steps should she carry out in order to prepare herself for the meeting?

Options:
1. She verifies her reservation of the meeting room that she chose
2. She tests the computer and projector that she plans to use in the meeting
3. She prints the annual report that she intends to cover in the meeting, preparing copies for participants
4. She reflects on the tension that exists between two attendees and plans how she'll guide any conflict positively
5. She ensures that everyone she's invited will attend the meeting
6. She clarifies the purpose of the meeting and makes sure that her objectives match it

Answer

Option 1: This option is correct. The venue in which you intend to hold your meeting should be verified as available and distraction free.

Option 2: This option is correct. Since time in a meeting is valuable, you should make sure that all your equipment is functioning properly beforehand.

Option 3: This option is correct. Any materials that you want to refer to in your meeting should be prepared and checked over in advance of the meeting.

Option 4: This option is correct. It's a good idea to consider the dynamics of the group you're meeting with so that you can anticipate any problems that may arise and think about how to steer them back to topic.

Option 5: This option is incorrect. Determining who is available for meetings is part of an earlier step in the process.

Option 6: This option is incorrect. Setting the meeting's purpose and objectives occurs much earlier in the preparation process.

Prepare others

As well as preparing yourself for the meeting, you need to prepare others. One way you can do this is to circulate the meeting's agenda well in advance of the meeting. Having access to the agenda allows participants to be clear about the purpose and objectives of the meeting. It also enables them to familiarize themselves with the issues to be addressed, or a particular task they've been assigned.

If the meeting is due to address a complex issue or controversial decision, you should consider some additional preparation.

You might have individuals or a group prepare a detailed analysis of the issue in advance. Try breaking the larger issue into its constituent parts.

Some important questions to ask might include, "What are some of the options available?" and "What will determine an effective solution?"

It's important to establish a set of guidelines to help maintain a respectful atmosphere. Guidelines are vital to the success of a meeting. They help minimize disruptions and confusion, while encouraging productive participation. There are two important varieties of guidelines you should establish for your meetings: roles and ground rules.

See each guideline to learn more about it.

Roles

It's helpful to assign someone to be a timekeeper to remind people of time limits. You may also want to appoint a meeting secretary who can record the meeting's proceedings.

Finally, make sure a chairperson has been assigned to lead the meeting. A lack of leadership in meetings can lead to one person taking over who may not be familiar with the goals of the meeting. The meeting's chair will also help determine who is entitled to speak, vote, and
make motions.

Ground rules

Ground rules are expectations for meeting behavior. They should reflect your groups's values and so should be decided upon together, if possible. Rules may include determining if meeting attendance is mandatory, as well as committing to arriving promptly and starting on time.

EFFECTIVE BUSINESS MEETINGS

Other ground rules may include allowing speakers to finish their thoughts, keeping discussions focused on topic, and avoiding personal conflicts.

You should make the ground rules clear to participants. You may circulate them with the agenda you send out, preview them at the beginning of the meeting, or even post them in the meeting room.

Isaac is holding a meeting at the end of the week. In order to prepare his team, he sends out the meeting's agenda at the beginning of the week.

In the e-mail, he asks two attendees if they'll prepare a report detailing a budget problem so that the team can spend time drafting conclusions. He also confirms if two others will serve as timekeeper and secretary, respectively.

Isaac also includes the team's most recent set of ground rules with the agenda.

It may be helpful for you to follow a checklist of the things you should do to prepare yourself and others for meetings.

Question
Alexandra is holding a meeting next week.
What examples reflect things she should do to prepare her attendees for the meeting?

Options:
1. She sends a copy of the meeting's agenda to everyone she's invited to the meeting
2. She asks everyone to summarize an aspect of a decision that needs to be made
3. She ensures that her appointed secretary and timekeeper can continue in their roles
4. She repeats the expectations they hold of each other at the beginning of the meeting
5. She writes a list of the behavior she will not tolerate in her meeting and e-mails it to the group
6. She calls a preliminary meeting to finalize the agenda

39

for the regularly scheduled meeting

Answer

Option 1: This option is correct. Circulating the meeting's agenda in advance gives participants a good idea of what to expect and an opportunity to prepare themselves for what will be covered.

Option 2: This option is correct. Complex or challenging issues may warrant more involved preparation. This can include asking attendees to prepare reports or analyses relevant to particular issues or decisions.

Option 3: This option is correct. It's important to establish clear roles for the meeting. Common roles include the meeting chair, secretary, and timekeeper.

Option 4: This option is correct. Establishing and reminding the group of ground rules that they've agreed upon helps ensure that an atmosphere of fairness and respect prevails over the meeting.

Option 5: This option is incorrect. While a set of ground rules is important for a meeting, they should reflect the values of the whole group and so be generated cooperatively, not solely by the meeting's leader.

Option 6: This option is incorrect. The agenda is part of the meeting leader's preparation, not the group's. It should be circulated in advance, but not decided on in a separate meeting.

Summary

The final step of preparing for an effective meeting is to ensure that you and your participants are ready. Preparing yourself includes making sure the venue is appropriate and available. Verify that any relevant equipment and materials are secured and in working order. Finally, consider the dynamics of the team and any problems that may arise.

Preparing others involves circulating the agenda in advance and taking a more involved approach to preparation if a particularly complex or controversial issue is on the meeting's agenda. Make sure that the meeting's guidelines are clear and establish roles for participants and ground rules for the meeting.

MANAGING EFFECTIVE BUSINESS MEETINGS

Have you ever attended a meeting that left you feeling frustrated? Perhaps the meeting was too long, unfocused, or dominated by arguments and disagreements. Not all meetings have to be like this. Meetings can be very productive; many issues can be resolved, and participants can feel grateful they attended.

So why does one meeting succeed and another one fail? The reason could be that some meeting leaders are unsure of their responsibilities at each stage of a business meeting. Perhaps the meeting leader's opening comments set the wrong tone, or maybe the discussion lost focus and was allowed to drift.

There are different types of meetings, but most follow a similar trajectory. Whether it's a regular meeting or a task force meeting, the meeting leader should open the meeting with appropriate information and in the right tone. An effective meeting leader encourages full participation from the group to ensure the objectives are reached within the allotted time. To close the meeting, the leader summarizes the decisions arrived at and follows up on the actions that need to be taken.

This course covers the skills and lessons that will help you to fulfill the key responsibilities of a meeting leader at each stage of a business meeting. You will learn about opening a meeting properly and closing it in the correct way. The course also demonstrates how to facilitate good decision-making during a meeting, as well as how to manage time in a meeting.

STARTING AND CONDUCTING A MEETING

Opening the meeting and setting the tone

Imagine you're a meeting leader. You've carried out the necessary steps to prepare for the meeting, such as finalizing the agenda, selecting the participants, and planning activities that will prompt discussion. In addition, you've confirmed that the audio-visual equipment you require is in place.

The meeting's participants have begun to arrive and it's one minute until the scheduled start of the meeting. The participants look toward you for direction. As meeting leader, where do you go from here?

Reflect

First, you should be aware of your core responsibilities as a meeting leader. From your own experiences as a meeting leader or as a participant in meetings, what do you think are the core responsibilities of a meeting leader?

Core responsibilities of a meeting leader

Your response may have listed some of these responsibilities. A meeting leader sets the tone of the meeting and encourages those in attendance to participate. The meeting leader is also responsible for facilitating a well-considered agreement through effective decision-making. Managing time and ensuring the agenda is followed are further responsibilities. In addition to ensuring that the work of the group is recorded and shared, the meeting leader ensures that there is follow-up on action items and next steps.

All meetings follow a series of basic steps, regardless of the purpose of the meeting. The first step is opening the meeting, and the second is conducting the meeting. The third step is closing the meeting. And the fourth step is following up the meeting. This topic covers the first two steps. The remaining steps are addressed in a later topic.

The first step – opening the meeting – is important because first impressions last. As a meeting leader, you should set a precedent by starting the meeting on time, even if some participants haven't arrived. This makes it clear that you're leading a focused and organized meeting.

There are three goals for opening a meeting: set a positive tone, review and confirm expectations for the meeting, and convey logistical information. Meeting leaders can achieve these goals with their opening comments.

The first goal of your opening is to set a positive tone. You need to create enthusiasm, interest, and appreciation among participants.

Opening with introductions can help establish the tone of the meeting. Attendees will be more comfortable once they know who you are and who everyone else is.

Using praise and appreciation is another way to set a positive tone. For example, depending on circumstances, you could mention that you appreciate everyone making it to the meeting despite the bad weather.

Another way to set the tone is to outline your hopes for the meeting. For instance, by saying that you hope the meeting will help generate new ideas for products or provide a solution to a longstanding problem, you're conveying a positive goal for the meeting.

The final action that you can take to set a positive tone is to request participants' help to make the meeting a success.

Again, this is about asserting a positive influence. By asking the participants to become actively involved in making the meeting a success, rather than being passive observers, you're getting off to the right start. To do this, you could ask attendees to help manage the group's time by sticking to the agenda.

Question
Which actions represent some of the core responsibilities of a meeting leader?
Options:
1. Setting the tone
2. Ensuring attendees participate only when asked to
3. Facilitating a well-considered agreement
4. Letting the agenda flow naturally without time limits
5. Ensuring that the work of the group is recorded and shared 6. Ensuring follow-up on action items and next steps
Answer

Option 1: *This option is correct. It's important for the meeting leader to set the correct tone because this will influence the outcome of the meeting.*

Option 2: *This option is incorrect. The meeting leader should ensure participation by encouraging attendees to contribute, rather than limiting their contributions.*

Option 3: *This option is correct. Meeting leaders should facilitate a well-considered agreement through effective decision-making.*

Option 4: *This option is incorrect. A meeting leader should manage time and ensure that the agenda is followed. Without time limits, the meeting could go on for too long or fail to address all the items on the agenda.*

Option 5: This option is correct. By ensuring that the work of the group is recorded and shared, the meeting leader is maximizing the benefits of what was achieved during the meeting.

Option 6: This option is correct. Ensuring follow-up on action items and next steps means that the meeting will not have been in vain.

Reviewing expectations and logistics

The second goal for opening a meeting is to review and confirm expectations for the meeting. This establishes what you want the meeting to accomplish, as well as how participants should conduct themselves during the meeting. You should state the purpose of the meeting during your opening comments. For example, you might state that you've scheduled this meeting to discuss an upcoming merger.

Agreeing on adjustments or last-minute additions to the agenda is another element of reviewing and confirming expectations for the meeting.

As the meeting leader, you can ask if the agenda is acceptable to all the participants. You should also ask if there are any last-minute additions to the agenda. Ideally, this action should be carried out in advance of the meeting itself. However, asking for final confirmation during your opening remarks is acceptable.

You should review the ground rules for the meeting. Examples of ground rules include asking that participants keep their comments brief, respect each other's opinions, and avoid raising new issues that aren't on the agenda.

Ground rules should be communicated to participants before the meeting starts. They can be circulated in an e-mail, posted on a notice board, or included as part of the agenda. Usually, it's not necessary to review ground rules in your opening comments, except in two instances.

If the meeting is the first time the group has gathered and you want to set the ground rules collaboratively, then they need to be reviewed.

And if there are specific ground rules that weren't followed particularly well in a previous meeting, they should be reviewed to encourage implementation.

The final goal for opening a meeting is to convey logistical information. As the meeting leader, you have the responsibility to make "housekeeping" announcements to inform the participants about details they will need to know in relation to the meeting or the venue.

This includes reviewing roles, such as who is the timekeeper and who will take the minutes of the meeting.

The "housekeeping" announcements are particularly important

if the meeting venue is unfamiliar to the participants. You should mention issues such as parking, restrooms, lunch rooms, and health and safety. Also, give details about handouts or other materials you intend to use during the meeting.

Question
When should ground rules be reviewed in a meeting leader's opening comments?
Options:
1. When the group is meeting for the first time
2. When the ground rules weren't followed in a previous meeting
3. When the group meets on a weekly basis
4. When the meeting leader wants to convey "housekeeping" information

Answer

Option 1: This option is correct. The ground rules should be reviewed when the group is meeting for the first time to allow for the rules to be agreed on in a collaborative way.

Option 2: This option is correct. The meeting leader should review the ground rules if they weren't properly followed in a previous meeting. By reviewing the ground rules, the meeting leader is re-emphasizing that these rules need to be followed.

Option 3: This option is incorrect. In this case, because the meeting takes place on a weekly basis, the participants will already be familiar with the ground rules.

Option 4: This option is incorrect. Reviewing ground rules has no connection to "housekeeping" information, which relates to the goal of conveying logistical information.

Gail is the marketing manager for a manufacturer of protective clothing. The company is expanding and hoping to enter new territories abroad. Gail has scheduled a meeting to discuss this issue. Every member of the Marketing Department is in attendance, including Mike. Some members of the company's Finance Department are also in attendance, including Kelly. Follow along as Gail uses her opening comments to set a positive tone, review

EFFECTIVE BUSINESS MEETINGS

and confirm expectations for the meeting, and convey logistical information.

Gail: Hi everyone. My colleagues from the Marketing Department will know who I am. However, for the benefit of members of the Finance Department who might not know me, my name is Gail and I'm the marketing manager. I appreciate that all of you have made the effort to get to this conference center, even though it's not centrally located.
Gail is friendly.

Kelly: Thanks for the welcome, Gail. *Kelly is friendly.*

Gail: I hope that when this meeting concludes, we'll have decided on a strategy for launching our products in several foreign markets. It will be very helpful if everyone is mindful of the time allocations for agenda items.
Gail is calm.

Mike: We'll make sure that we don't go over our time limits. *Mike is focused.*

Gail: Thanks, Mike. This meeting has been scheduled to specifically discuss how we can export our products that are aimed at the construction industry. I hope you've all had a chance to review the agenda. Is there anything that anyone would like to add to it?
Gail is friendly.

Kelly: I noticed that the agenda doesn't cover the issue of dealing with varying tax legislation in different territories. I think this is an important finance issue.
Kelly is serious.

Gail: Yes, I agree. Let's add it to the agenda as the last item for discussion. Before we proceed, since this is the first time that both departments have met together, we should go over some ground rules. Please respect each other's opinions, and only one person should speak at any one time. Is that OK? Also, I forgot to ask someone to take the minutes of the meeting.
Gail is earnest.

Mike: The ground rules sound fair to me. I can take the minutes, if it will help.
Mike is friendly and eager.

Gail: Thanks, Mike. Before we move on – just so you all know – the restrooms are located off the main corridor on the left. You'll also see that I've provided each of you with a report that includes some useful analysis about some of the markets that we're targeting.

Gail is happy.

Gail set a positive tone for the meeting in her opening comments. She then reviewed and confirmed expectations for the meeting and conveyed logistical information that the participants needed to know.

Question
Match each example of an opening statement to the goal it serves. Each goal may have more than one match.

Options:
1. "Before the introductions, I'd like to thank you for attending, given the weather."
2. "I hope this meeting will resolve our recruitment issues."
3. "Let's quickly review the group's satisfaction with the agenda."
4. "We squabbled at our previous meeting. During this one, please respect each other."
5. "Before we review who's going to act as timekeeper, I'd like to point out the fire exits."

Targets:
1. Setting a positive tone
2. Reviewing and confirming expectations
3. Conveying logistical information

Answer

Acknowledging attendance is an example of a statement that sets a positive tone. Meeting leaders use introductions and praise and appreciation to achieve this goal. Stating that resolving a recruitment issue is the aim of the meeting is an example of how a meeting leader can outline the hopes for a meeting.

Discussing the group's attitude toward the agenda is an example of a statement that reviews and confirms expectations for the meeting. To achieve this goal, a meeting leader's opening statement should state the purpose of the meeting, seek agreement on adjustments and additions to the agenda, and review ground rules, if necessary. Mentioning that respect is an issue is an example of reviewing ground rules.

Pointing out the fire exits is an example of a statement a meeting leader may use to achieve the goal of conveying logistical information. Team leaders review roles, make "housekeeping" announcements, and describe handouts and materials to achieve this goal.

Conducting the meeting

As a meeting leader, you should be aware of what type of meeting you're conducting. This is the second step in leading a meeting. Meetings can be put into one of two categories, depending on their purpose: regular meetings, or task force meetings.

See each meeting category to learn more about it.

Regular meetings

This type of meeting happens on a recurring basis. It's suitable for sharing information and reviewing issues. Meetings in this category include staff meetings, management meetings, political councils, and board meetings. The participants of these meetings are the members of the designated group. For example, a board meeting's participants would be members of the board.

A meeting in this category is usually led by the participant in the most senior position. In this respect, regular meetings have a top-down authority structure. Regular meetings aren't suitable for finding solutions to complex problems.

Task force meetings

A task force meeting is convened with a specific purpose in mind. This type of meeting operates at a higher level of analysis than a regular meeting. Task force meetings are suitable for solving complex problems and devising strategies. Attendees at task force meetings are usually experts in their chosen areas.

Task force meetings are democratic in nature, with equality among participants. Rather than having a traditional leader, task force meetings have a facilitator who guides and coordinates the meeting.

Consider an example of a regular meeting. A medium-sized food processing company convenes a weekly management meeting. All members of the company's management structure are required to attend.

The meetings are used to discuss day-to-day decisions that concern the running of the company. This usually involves issues concerning equipment, employees, suppliers, and customers.

The meeting is led by the most senior manager in the company.

Now consider this example of a task force meeting. A biopharmaceutical company convenes a task force meeting to analyze why the company's new product to treat arthritis isn't proving effective in testing.

This is a complex issue and the company's leading scientists, pharmacists, and biopharmaceutical engineers attend to find a solution.

The meeting leader is the head of the Research and Development Department. He isn't the participant with the most senior position. Rather, he's been appointed because his department maintains contact with all the other departments in the company.

There are five common steps for completing agenda items for both regular and task force meetings. The first step is to state the topic. The second step is to describe the process and time frame for covering the topic. The third step is to encourage participation and discussion, and the fourth step is to get agreement. Finally, the fifth step is to move on to the next agenda item.

Step three, encouraging participation and discussion, is a more complex process in a task force meeting than a regular meeting, because of the high level of analysis required. In task force meetings, step three has several substeps. The first substep is to identify the desired outcome, and the second substep is to define and analyze the problem. The third substep is to generate possible solutions. And the final substep is to evaluate the options and then choose the best solution.

See each substep that applies to task force meetings to learn more about it.

3a. Identify the desired outcome
It's important to identify the desired outcome so that participants can visualize what success looks like and then set suitable goals and objectives to achieve it.

3b. Define and analyze the problem
Defining and analyzing the problem involves gathering intelligence and the relevant data so that the task force participants can identify and relate to the problem as a collective.

3c. Generate possible solutions
This substep prompts attendees to generate multiple ideas and possible solutions. This is part of a diligent approach that considers all options.

3d. Evaluate and choose the best solution
Once the potential solutions have been identified, they're rigorously evaluated and scrutinized. Only the best solutions are chosen.

These substeps apply to task force meetings only; they don't relate to regular meetings. The first two substeps – identify the desired outcome, and define and analyze the problem – are necessary to get task force meeting participants to share their understanding of the problem and to expose assumptions and possible constraints.

Question
Which steps relate to both task force and regular meetings?
Options:
1. State the topic
2. Describe the process and time frame 3. Encourage participation and discussion 4. Get agreement
5. Move on to the next agenda item
6. Identify the desired outcome
7. Define and analyze the problems
Answer

Option 1: This option is correct. Stating the topic is the first step in the process for completing agenda items.

Option 2: This option is correct. Describing the process and time frame is the second step in the process for completing agenda items.

Option 3: This option is correct. Encouraging participation and discussion is the third step in the process for completing agenda items.

Option 4: This option is correct. Getting agreement is the fourth step in the process for completing agenda items.

Option 5: This option is correct. Moving on to the next agenda item is the fifth step in the process for completing agenda items.

Option 6: This option is incorrect. Identifying the desired outcome is a substep of encouraging participation and discussion. It relates to task force meetings only.

Option 7: This option is incorrect. Defining and analyzing the problems is a substep of encouraging participation and discussion. It relates to task force meetings only.

Summary

A meeting leader can achieve three goals by using the right statements to open a meeting. The first goal is setting a positive tone, and the second is reviewing and confirming expectations for the meeting. The final goal is conveying logistical information.

There are five common steps that are followed to complete agenda items in both regular and task force meetings: state the topic; describe the process and time frame for covering the topic; encourage participation and discussion; get agreement; and finally, move on to the next agenda item.

FACILITATING GOOD DECISION-MAKING IN A MEETING

Decision-making and participation

Meetings play an important role in day-to-day business. They involve discussing issues and making decisions. The process for completing agenda items in a meeting includes steps that focus on encouraging participation and discussion, and getting agreement. These steps play an integral part in helping participants make the correct decisions.

The first step for completing agenda items is to state the topic. The second step is to describe the process and time frame for covering the topic. The third step is to encourage participation and discussion. The fourth step is to get agreement. The final step is to move on to the next agenda item.

Reflect
What do you think are the criteria for making a good decision?

Your answer may have included some of the criteria for making a good decision:
- it supports organizational needs
- it's in the best interests of the stakeholders
- it's beneficial in the short and long terms
- it's realistic and possible to implement
- it focuses on root causes rather than symptoms
- it's aware of impact on resources

- it reflects creative and holistic thinking, and
- it questions entrenched traditions

There are three key responsibilities that a meeting leader should be aware of to facilitate good decision-making in a meeting. The first is to encourage full participation. The second is to document and display accomplishments as the meeting progresses. And the third is to implement the right decision-making approach.

The first responsibility is encouraging full participation. This requires you to ensure everyone attending the meeting is given the chance to contribute to the discussion.

You should create an environment that welcomes, rather than discourages, participation. If attendees don't get the opportunity to contribute to a meeting, they may become frustrated or resentful.

You should be careful that you don't alienate or embarrass participants for their contribution, even if the comment seemed foolish or irrelevant. Similarly, you shouldn't allow a person's contribution to be trivialized by other members of the group.

You can encourage participation by communicating the value of analyzing an issue from different perspectives. Urge people to state their opinions, or deliberately make a statement that you know will provoke a reaction from the group.

If some people at the meeting are quiet, consider asking them a question directly. To make sure that participants who aren't vocally active in the meeting are following what's going on, ask all attendees to take notes.

Another strategy that encourages participation is to use group techniques that solicit the input of all participants.

There are many group techniques you can use to encourage participation. Brainstorming is particularly useful because it helps people think of innovative ideas without being constrained by practicalities. In a brainstorming session, participants are encouraged to think creatively and share their ideas as soon as they occur.

Question

Based on what you've learned, which statements are likely to effectively encourage full participation in a meeting?
Options:
1. "That relates to another issue, but thanks for the input."
2. "OK, I'm looking forward to hearing what all of you have to say about this problem."
    3. "Simon, I'd like to hear your opinion on this subject."
    4. "In this brainstorming session, I'm going to ask each of you to reveal what your first impression of the issue was."
    5. "That's quite an amusing point, but it's of no use to this discussion."
    6. "I take it that those of you who are silent consent to the decision."

Answer

Option 1: This option is correct. A meeting leader shouldn't make a participant feel uncomfortable for making an irrelevant comment.

Option 2: This option is correct. It's important that a meeting leader emphasizes the value of looking at an issue from different perspectives.

Option 3: This option is correct. If a member of the group is quiet or not contributing, the meeting leader should directly attempt to involve the person in the discussion.

Option 4: This option is correct. Using a group technique such as brainstorming is an effective method for soliciting each participant's opinion.

Option 5: This option is incorrect. Meeting leaders should encourage input from participants and not embarrass anyone. Meeting leaders should also ensure that they don't allow participants to trivialize someone else's contribution.

Option 6: This option is incorrect. It's important for a meeting leader to prompt discussion, rather than accepting the reluctance of some participants to contribute.

Documenting accomplishments

Documenting and displaying accomplishments as the meeting progresses is the second key responsibility. Participants need to be able to see important points documented in a visual way. You can use projectors, whiteboards, or flip charts to display this information.

By displaying recorded information during a meeting, you'll help participants make a more informed decision.

Another benefit of this approach is that participants who are unsure of an important part of the discussion can refer to the displayed material and ask questions.

Recording information and displaying it also helps to outline in a clear, linear way what has been determined and accomplished in the meeting so far.

There are two types of information that should be displayed during a meeting. The first is information relating to agreements and decisions. The second is information relating to action items.

It's important to display information relating to agreements and decisions because it helps keep the meeting focused. It also ensures that a decision that's already been made isn't unnecessarily revisited.

Information relating to action items should be recorded and displayed separately. Once an action item has been agreed upon, you should record a description of what it involves, who will carry it out, a date of completion, and details of any extra resources that will be required to complete it.

For example, Jane works in the IT Department of a government agency. She's the leader of a task force meeting convened to discuss upgrading the agency's current software.

As the meeting progresses, Jane documents and displays agreements the group has made. For instance, she writes "Software to be developed in-house" on the whiteboard as one of the agreements.

The group decides that a provisional budget for the software upgrade project needs to be drafted. Jane uses a flip chart to document this action item. She records that this task will be assigned to her colleague Sue, its due date is two weeks from now, and no extra resources will be required.

Question
How does displaying recorded information during a meeting help improve decision-making?

Options:
1. It captures issues, constraints, and assumptions
2. It encourages clarification
3. It organizes the discussion
4. It allows participants to observe instead of contribute
5. It prevents disagreements

Answer

Option 1: *This option is correct. Displaying recorded information during a meeting does capture issues, constraints, and assumptions. This information can help participants make more informed decisions.*

Option 2: *This option is correct. As information is being displayed, participants who may be*
unsure about certain items have an opportunity to seek clarification.

Option 3: *This option is correct. Displaying recorded information does play an organizational function. Meeting participants can clearly see what has been accomplished and what action items have been determined.*

Option 4: *This option is incorrect. The purpose of displaying recorded information isn't to allow participants to become passive. Effective decision-making requires participants to contribute different perspectives.*

Option 5: *This option is incorrect. Displaying recorded information isn't supposed to prevent disagreements. Sometimes the most valuable perspective or idea can be generated by participants disagreeing with each other.*

The right decision-making approach

Implementing the right decision-making approach is the third key responsibility. There are four different approaches to decision-making: the expert style, the consultative style, the majority style, and the consensus style.

As a meeting leader, the decision-making style you choose de-

pends on certain criteria:
- how much time is available to you
- the importance of the issue
- the importance of participant buy-in, and
- the expertise and knowledge of the participants

As with each of the decision-making approaches, the expert style requires that you are aware of the considerations regarding its use. You should also know when and how to use this particular style.

See each item to learn more about the considerations of using the expert style, when to use it, and how to use it.

Considerations of use

The expert style is one of the most traditional ways of making a decision. The decision is made by an expert or authority figure. This approach represents a quick and decisive action. However, the quality of the decision depends on the knowledge of a single decison-maker. The expert style doesn't use or develop the problem-solving or decision-making skills of the group.

When to use

The expert style is most effectively used in situations where time is short and there isn't extensive expertise available to consult with. This style should be used sparingly.

How to use

When using the expert style, it's advisable that the decision-maker explains the reasons for choosing a particular course of action and the impact it's likely to have. This helps participants understand the decision and makes them feel connected to the process.

For example, a financial controller for a freight company could say to participants of a meeting, "I've decided to reduce overtime to address the budget deficit. This decision won't be popular with our employees, but a cut has to be made somewhere."

The second decision-making approach involves the consultative style. It's similar to the expert style because the expert or authority figure retains the right to make the decision. But in the consultative style, the decision is made after the authority figure gathers input from others.

The consultative style takes time to implement. But it's typically worth it, because this approach usually results in better buy-in and increased satisfaction on the part of the other participants.

This style should be used when greater participant buy-in is required, but time is short. It's also suitable for use in situations where participants don't have the authority or expertise to reach a final decision.

To use this style, the expert should demonstrate a genuine desire for participants to contribute their views. It's also important to discuss the impact the decision will have on participants.

For example, an engineering expert working for a car manufacturing company may say, "Having listened to what you've all said, I've decided that we need to redesign the fuel injection system. This will mean that we'll have some very frustrating months ahead of us."

The majority style is the third decision-making approach. This style involves putting decisions to a vote, with the majority winning. It can result in a quick decision, but it can also cause divisions within a group. Also, participants may vote against their true opinions if they think they won't win the vote.

This style should be used when a meeting leader wants to gauge participants' views on less important decisions. The majority style is suitable for getting quick decisions and in situations when it's not important that all participants agree.

You should use this style when the group has to vote on a number of separate issues. If peer pressure is a concern, a secret ballot can be used. Consider an example of a statement from a meeting leader using this style: "Let's break this issue down into three separate votes. First, we'll vote on the procurement issue. Then we'll put the marketing strategy to a vote. Finally, we'll vote on the sales strategy."

Question

Match the decision-making style to the description of when it should be used.

Options:

A. Expert style

B. Consultative style C. Majority style

Targets:

1. When time is short and there's not much specialist advice available
2. When group members don't have the authority or expertise to reach a final decision
3. When a team leader wants to measure the group's point of view on several issues

Answer

The expert style should be used when there's limited time and when expert advice isn't readily accessible.

The consultative style should be used when a team leader wants to achieve better buy-in from the group. This style is also used when participants can't come to a common agreement.

The majority style is used to gauge where people stand on decisions. It's also used when it doesn't matter if the group members all agree or not.

The consensus style is the fourth decision-making approach. This style is used to reach a decision that all participants can live with and support, even though the agreement might not be unanimous. This means that the decision must not contravene a participant's beliefs or ethics.

The consensus style should be used when the issue being discussed is important and requires that the views of all participants be expressed. This style can be used in situations where a meeting leader needs to have all participants on board with the decision.

For this style to be effective, all participants should speak their minds. You should encourage clarifying questions so that group members understand each other's points of view. You should also make sure that the group understands the decision that's being discussed.

When using the consensus style, you should synthesize ideas by combining important elements of each idea to form a single coherent message. This can make the decision more acceptable to some participants without alienating others.

Here's an example of a statement a meeting leader could make to synthesize several ideas: "We should look at the planned expansion of our manufacturing facilities, administrative headquarters, and dispatch depots in the context of the company's overall restructuring program."

It's important to implement a time limit when using the consensus style. Meeting leaders should be prepared to switch to another decision-making process if consensus can't be reached.

Question

As a meeting leader, you want to maximize participation and ensure that all participants express their views and buy in to decisions that are made in a meeting.

Which statements would achieve this?

Options:
1. "I think you might be confusing two different issues, but your input is welcome."
2. "For this meeting to be effective, I need to hear your opinions."
3. "If you need clarification on what we discuss, please be sure to ask me questions."
4. "Reaching consensus is comparable to reaching an agreement we can all live with."
5. "I can't believe you said that – this meeting is for adults."
6. "We can reach consensus quicker if we analyze issues on an individual basis."

Answer

Option 1: *This option is correct. To encourage participation, meeting leaders should avoid embarrassing participants who make irrelevant comments.*

Option 2: *This option is correct. By asking group members to offer* their opinions, a meeting leader can encourage participation.

Option 3: This option is correct. Encouraging the use of clarifying questions can help a group to reach consensus.

Option 4: This option is correct. Making sure that participants understand what consensus is will help the group buy in to the decision.

Option 5: This option is incorrect. Embarrassing a group member discourages participation. **Option 6:** This option is incorrect. Consensus is better achieved when issues are analyzed together.

Summary

There are three key responsibilities that a meeting leader should be aware of to facilitate good decision-making in a meeting. The first is to encourage full participation. The second is to document and display accomplishments as the meeting progresses. And the third is to implement the right decision-making approach.

Four styles can be used to implement the right decision-making approach: the expert style, the consultative style, the majority style, and the consensus style.

MANAGING TIME IN A MEETING

Diagnosing drift in a meeting

The ultimate goal of any meeting is to address each item on the agenda. But as a meeting leader, you also need to end the meeting on time. It's very frustrating for participants when a meeting runs over its schedule, because it will impact the rest of their working day. When you end a meeting on time, attendees appreciate that you respect their time.

You can achieve the meeting goal – within the allocated time – by sticking to the agenda and the time line. You should control the pace of the meeting without restricting the attendees' right to voice their opinions.

As meeting leader, you have a number of responsibilities. You should keep time, prevent the discussion from drifting, and make changes to the schedule if necessary.

To keep time in a meeting, you can appoint one of the participants as the timekeeper. This person is responsible for keeping you informed of the amount of time that's left for each agenda item.

For example, the assigned timekeeper might indicate to you that the current agenda item being discussed has already exceeded half its allotted time.

You then can announce to the group that the allotted space on the agenda for the item is nearing an end, so it's time to begin to conclude this part of the meeting.

Another of your responsibilities as meeting leader is to prevent the discussion from drifting away from the meeting's purpose. Drifting is when the discussion goes "off topic" and is no longer relevant to the agenda item's original purpose. The most common causes of drift include unclear objectives, participants wanting to discuss other issues, participants arguing excessively, and participants getting distracted by something else.

See each cause of drift in a meeting to learn more about it.

Unclear objectives

In a meeting, if the objectives are unclear, participants can become involved in irrelevant discussions or raise points that are unrelated to the meeting.

For instance, suppose the objective of a meeting to discuss a footwear manufacturer's new range of running shoes is to identify the most suitable target demographic. But some of the participants aren't aware of this objective. As a result, they begin to discuss the unit cost of

manufacturing the product, rather than discussing the most suitable consumer market to sell the product in.

Participants want to discuss other issues

A meeting can drift when participants want to discuss other issues. A participant may want to raise an issue that isn't on the agenda.

Consider the example of a meeting that has been convened to discuss an engineering company's equipment procurement strategy. The discussion has focused on what physical equipment the company will need to purchase to be able to complete next year's customer orders. However, one participant insists on discussing design software packages. The meeting loses focus because of this.

Participants argue excessively

When participants argue and bicker excessively, it can cause the meeting to drift off course.

For example, an insurance company's Sales Department is discussing sales targets in a meeting. The subject of sales leads is raised. Two participants begin to argue over how the leads are distributed. The argument continues and other participants become involved. The focus of the meeting switches from sales targets to favoritism within the department.

Participants are distracted

Participants can become easily distracted. It's very difficult for meeting leaders to completely avoid this.

Here's an example. Several managers from a large pharmaceutical company are attending a meeting to discuss quality control issues. The venue is a hotel conference room. Halfway through the meeting, a very noisy crowd can be heard cheering and clapping outside the conference room. A wedding reception has been scheduled for the same day. The meeting participants are distracted and begin to discuss weddings rather than the items on the agenda.

In your role as a meeting leader, it's important that you're able to diagnose what causes drift in a meeting. You should be aware of the impact that unclear objectives, discussing other issues, excessive arguing, and distractions can have on a group.

Question
Match the examples of drift in a meeting to what causes them.
Options:
A. Lisa discusses life insurance policies because it wasn't clear that the meeting was meant to discuss health insurance policies
B. A meeting to discuss a food retailer's waste policy loses focuses when a participant insists on discussing a nonagenda item
C. A prolonged disagreement between two accountants over a tax issue disrupts a meeting
D. Participants discussing a soft drink company's marketing strategy lose focus because the meeting room is adjacent to a road with heavy traffic
Targets:
1. Unclear objectives
2. Participants discussing other issues 3. Participants arguing excessively
4. Participants being distracted

Answer

Discussing an irrelevant issue, such as life insurance during a meeting about health insurance, is an example of drift in a meeting caused by participants not being sure of the objectives.

Raising nonagenda items is an example of drift caused by participants wanting to discuss other items.

A meeting being disrupted by constant bickering about a tax issue is an example of drift caused by participants arguing excessively.

Participants losing focus because of constant heavy traffic on a nearby road is an example of drift in a meeting caused by attendees being distracted.

Addressing drift during a meeting

As a meeting leader, you're probably going to have to deal with meeting drift sometimes. Your response should aim to get the meeting back on track and ensure the meeting addresses each agenda item.

When a conversation in a meeting drifts because the objectives are unclear, you should clarify the objectives and make sure that all the participants fully understand them.

When a participant brings up an irrelevant point, you should intervene as soon as you can.

To address this issue, you could say something like, "Sorry folks, I guess I haven't made the objective clear. Let me restate it."

When drifting is caused by participants wanting to discuss other issues, your responses should make it clear that these issues aren't relevant to the meeting.

For example, you could say, "That issue isn't related to the subject of this meeting."

If the issue turns out to be unrelated, you should suggest that it be "parked" in the "parking lot." The parking lot is a concept where any ideas, issues, or suggestions that are off topic are recorded on a flip chart. The chart should be located to one side of the room so that it doesn't distract the group. Items that have been "parked" can be discussed after all the other agenda items, or added to the agenda for the next meeting.

EFFECTIVE BUSINESS MEETINGS

Participants arguing excessively is one of the most common causes of drift in a meeting. As a meeting leader, your responses should be impartial. Don't take sides in the argument.

Give the arguing participants an opportunity to make their cases. You can then ask the other participants for their opinions.

You could respond to this type of situation by saying to those who are arguing, "We want to hear what both of you have to say. But the rest of the group will also have their say."

Finally, drift situations can also occur when participants are distracted.

If the group does become distracted, you can pause for a short period and then resume the meeting. For example, you could say, "Let's take a five minute breather."

Don't try to compete with the distraction. You should acknowledge it, then provide a quick recap of what's been said and move on with the meeting. Use humor if appropriate.

Question
Match each situation where drift has occurred in a discussion to the proper response a meeting leader should make to address it.

Options:
1. A discussion goes off topic because a participant discusses an objective in the wrong context
2. The meeting drifts because some members of the group want to introduce nonagenda items
3. Two participants in a meeting constantly disagree with each other
4. A man wearing headphones, who is unwittingly singing loudly, distracts participants as he walks by the conference room

Targets:
1. "Before we go on, I think it's a good time to review the objectives of this meeting."
2. "Those issues don't relate to the purpose of this meeting, but let's park them for later discussion."
3. "OK, both of you should outline your positions and then

we'll see what the rest of the group thinks."
4. "Another star is born! Let's recap what we've covered so far."

Answer

This is an example of a response a meeting leader makes when unclear objectives cause a participant to discuss an issue in the wrong context.

This is an example of a suitable reply from a meeting leader when the discussion drifts because participants want to introduce nonagenda items.

This response is a suitable reply for a meeting leader to make when participants disagree constantly and create a drift situation.

This an example of a response a meeting leader could use to address a drift situation caused by participants becoming distracted by a man singing to himself.

Getting a discussion back on track

Your third responsibility as meeting leader is to make changes to the schedule if necessary. This situation usually occurs when the time allocated for discussing an agenda item proves to have been underestimated. More time is needed, but this could jeopardize the meeting by going over the scheduled time.

There are some options available to you to deal with this type of situation. You can cut the discussion short, table later items, or reschedule the current discussion for another meeting.

When you consider the options for changing the meeting schedule, you should be aware that each one should be used under specific conditions.

See each option to learn when it should be used.

Cut discussion short

If the current issue under discussion is close to closure, you should wrap up the conversation and move on to the next item on the agenda.

Table later items

You should table items that appear later on the agenda to allow the current discussion to reach closure. Tabling an item means that you suspend discussing it. This is particularly important if later items require the current issue to be finalized before they can be addressed.

Reschedule current discussion

When there are other, more pressing agenda items waiting to be discussed, you should reschedule the item currently being discussed for another meeting.

It will be up to you as meeting manager to make the right decisions to change the schedule once you've assessed the situation.

Question

Match each circumstance for changing the schedule with the decision it relates to. Not all circumstances will match.

Options:

A. The issue being discussed has nearly been finalized
B. There are later agenda items that require the current issue to be finalized C. There are other more important items further down the agenda
D. The meeting room is needed by another group

Targets:

1. Cut discussion short
2. Table later items
3. Reschedule current discussion

Answer

When the item under discussion has nearly reached closure, this is an example of a situation where the meeting leader can cut the discussion short.

When there are later agenda items that require the current issue to be finalized before they
can be discussed, the later items should tabled.

When there are more important items further down the agenda, this is an example of when a meeting leader can reschedule the current discussion to another meeting.

Beth is leading a meeting at the e-commerce consultancy firm where she works. The meeting's objective is to discuss marketing opportunities that the company can advise its clients about. Both Nick and June are participants in the meeting, along with several others. The discussion has begun to drift because Nick and June have been arguing over whether or not to advise the company's clients to establish data mining functions. Follow along as Beth – in her role as meeting leader – responds to this situation.

Beth: Both of you seem to be passionate about this issue. We'll hear what both of you have to say, but the rest of the group will have an opportunity to voice their opinions as well.

Beth is composed.

Nick: Well, I think that data mining represents a great opportunity for some of our clients to increase their sales. Our clients can use the information they collect to formulate targeted sales strategies.

Nick is confident.

Beth: OK, thanks Nick. June, let's hear from you. *Beth is friendly.*

June: I disagree with Nick. I think that we should be very careful about advising our clients to establish data mining functions. Many people have concerns about how their personal information is stored and used online. I believe that if we advise our clients to focus on data mining, they may experience negative feedback from their customers.

June is concerned.

Beth: Thanks guys – both of you have made valid points. Let's see what the rest of the group thinks. Does anyone have any thoughts about what we've just heard?

Beth is enthusiastic.

To address the drift situation in the meeting, Beth gave both Nick and June an opportunity to make their cases. She then called on the other participants to contribute their opinions on the data mining issue. This was the correct response from Beth.

The meeting involving Beth, Nick, and June has moved on to another agenda item. The discussion is now focused on how the company can help its clients take advantage of social media opportunities. All the participants are making valuable contributions and definite progress is being made. But Beth realizes that she hasn't assigned enough time to adequately discuss this agenda item. Follow along as she makes a decision to change the schedule.

Beth: We've made excellent progress on this issue. Does anyone have any concluding remarks to add?

Beth is calm.

June: I think we've covered all the important points. We can begin to draw up some suggestions for our clients.

June is enthusiastic.

Nick: From what we've discussed so far, I'm confident that we can formulate an effective social media strategy. But I think we need to discuss our clients' willingness to embrace social media platforms in more detail.

Nick is determined.

Beth: I can appreciate that, Nick. But we've discussed that issue, although perhaps not in as much detail as you'd like. However, I think we're near the end of this issue, so I'd like to move on to the next item on the agenda.

Beth is authoritative.

Beth realized that the meeting was in jeopardy because she'd underestimated the length of time it would take to discuss the social media agenda item. She cut the discussion short because most of the valid points regarding the item had been covered. This was the appropriate decision for the circumstances.

Case Study: Question 1 of 2

Scenario

For your convenience, the case study is repeated with each question.

Roger is a meeting leader with a software development company. The objective of the meeting is to discuss a recent contract the company has been awarded to develop a new payroll system for a government department.

Help Roger get the discussion back on track and make the right decision about changing the schedule by answering the questions in order.

Question

The participants are distracted by the sound of an ambulance siren outside.

What should Roger say to get the meeting back on track?

Options:
1. "Let me just remind everyone that our purpose here is to discuss the new contract."
2. "I'm not sure if that issue is relevant."
3. "We can hear what both of you have to say and then decide."
4. "OK, let's just wait a minute until the ambulance has passed."

Answer

Option 1: *This option is incorrect. The participants were distracted rather than being unsure of the objectives, so Roger should pause the discussion to get the meeting back on track.*

Option 2: *This option is incorrect. The participants were distracted rather than trying to raise other issues. Roger should pause the discussion to get the meeting back on track.*

Option 3: *This option is incorrect. The group was distracted rather than arguing with each other. Roger should pause the discussion to get the meeting back on track.*

Option 4: *This is the correct option. Roger should pause the discussion to get the meeting back on track. He shouldn't try to compete with the distraction.*

Case Study: Question 2 of 2

Scenario

For your convenience, the case study is repeated with each question.

Roger is a meeting leader with a software development company. The objective of the meeting is to discuss a recent contract the company has been awarded to develop a new payroll system for a government department.

Help Roger get the discussion back on track and make the right decision about changing the schedule by answering the questions in order.

Question

The discussion is going well. The group is debating whether the customer's operating system can support the software package the company has in mind. Roger is concerned that not enough time has been allocated to discuss this issue. Later agenda items include provision of training to the client's employees and how long the installation process will take.

What decision should Roger make to change the schedule?

Options:

1. Cut the discussion short
2. Table later items
3. Reschedule the current discussion

Answer

Option 1: *This option is incorrect. There's no point in cutting the discussion short because the later agenda items can't be discussed until the operating system issue is resolved. Roger should table later items instead.*

Option 2: *This is the correct option. The later items can't be resolved until the current operating system issue is resolved.*

Option 3: *This option is incorrect. Roger shouldn't reschedule the current discussion because the later agenda items can't be discussed until the operating system issue is resolved. Roger should table later items instead.*

Summary

As meeting leader, it's your responsibility to keep time, prevent the discussion from drifting, and make changes to the schedule if necessary. To keep time in a meeting, you can appoint one of the participants as the timekeeper.

When you sense that the discussion is drifting, your response should aim to get the meeting back on track and ensure the meeting addresses each agenda item.

To make changes to the schedule, you can cut the discussion short, table later items, or reschedule the current discussion to another meeting.

ENDING A MEETING

Closing a meeting
After conducting the meeting, you need to bring it to a smooth and logical close, the third step that meetings follow. You should know when to close the meeting and how to send participants away with a positive feeling that reflects their satisfaction with what they've accomplished in the meeting. There are two reasons for closing a meeting. The first is that you reach the end of the agenda. The second is that you run out of time.

There are four steps that a meeting follows. The first step is opening the meeting. The second is conducting the meeting. The third step is closing the meeting. And the fourth step is following up the meeting.

Reaching the end of the agenda is the first reason for closing a meeting. Once all the agenda items have been properly addressed, it's time to bring proceedings to a close.
You shouldn't end a meeting by saying that there's time for one more question. This could lead to overruns that throw the participants' schedules into disarray.
After the last agenda item has been discussed, you've got a logical opportunity to bring the meeting to an end. There's no need to complicate matters by inviting further contributions from the group.
The other instance when you should close a meeting is when you run out of time.
You must end the meeting on time, every time. You should be conscious of time management during the meeting to ensure that the group has the chance to address as much of the agenda as possible.

EFFECTIVE BUSINESS MEETINGS

By ending the meeting on time, you send a clear message that you respect the participants' time. Even if some participants would rather keep the meeting open to discuss certain issues, you should stand firm and close the meeting.

One of your main aims as a meeting leader is to make the participants feel that the meeting was worthwhile. Participants should feel productive and have a clear sense of what needs to be done next.

There are several steps that you can follow to achieve this:
1. restate the objective of the meeting
2. summarize what was accomplished in the meeting
3. thank participants for attending and for their contributions
4. review the next steps, such as action items, assignments, parked items, and the details of the next meeting, and
5. evaluate the success of the meeting and collect lessons learned

Question

What are the correct situations for closing a meeting?

Options:
1. After the final agenda item has been discussed
2. After the agenda items have been discussed and one last question is asked
3. After the allocated time for the meeting has run out
4. After further issues are discussed when the scheduled time for the meeting has run out

Answer

Option 1: *This option is correct. As soon as the last agenda item has been addressed, it's time to close the meeting.*

Option 2: *This option is incorrect. Allowing one last question to be discussed after the last agenda item could cause costly, unnecessary, and unexpected time delays for participants.*

Option 3: This option is correct. Closing a meeting when the time has run out shows that a meeting leader respects the participants' time.

Option 4: This option is incorrect. A meeting leader shouldn't allow additional items to be discussed after the time has run out. This could create inconvenient delays for many participants.

Following up a meeting

Following up a meeting is the fourth and final step you need to complete in your role as meeting leader. To complete this step, you should send a record of the meeting around, follow up on actions taken, and inform attendees of progress made.

You can circulate the meeting minutes to ensure all the attendees have a record of the meeting. The minutes, which are often referred to as the meeting record, document the work that was accomplished during the meeting, including follow-up work that's required and action items that have been decided upon. Distributing the minutes helps prevent disagreements later. Also, the minutes provide group members with an indication of how effective they were at achieving objectives.

The meeting minutes are usually finalized when the meeting is over and then sent to each participant. The minutes should record the date and time of the meeting, who attended, what topics were discussed, the results of discussions, the action items decided on, and information about the next meeting.

See each item from the minutes to learn more about it.

Date and time of meeting

The date and time at which the meeting was held should be included in the minutes. For example, 2:00 p.m. on June 1.

Who attended

The names and positions of people who attended the meeting should be listed. For instance, "John, HR manager."

Topics discussed

The minutes should list all the topics that were discussed at the meeting. For example, these could include budgetary measures, payroll issues, and recruitment drives.

Results of discussion
The minutes should includes agreements, conclusions, and decisions. It's important that the minutes reflect what the actual decisions are, rather than how they were arrived at. Consider an example: "it has been decided to purchase added computer servers to back-up the company's operating system."

Action items
For each action item, the minutes should note who has been assigned to carry it out, when it's due to be completed, and what extra resources are required to carry it out. For example, an action item could be getting quotes from building contractors for renovations to the reception area. This task has been assigned to Sue. She has one month to complete the task, and she requires no extra resources to complete it.

Information about next meeting
The minutes should include information about the next meeting, including the date and time. For example, the next meeting is scheduled for 3:00 p.m. on August 1. If preliminary items for discussion at the next meeting have been agreed, they should be listed in the minutes also.

You should make sure that the minutes are objective and reflect fact, rather than opinion. Don't allow ambiguous or subjective language to be used. The minutes should be accurate, and clear and easy to follow. The best approach to minute-taking is to create a process that incorporates the group's agreed standards for what is to be included and apply it consistently.

To follow up on actions taken, you should first confirm the actions in writing with the people assigned to them. You then have to get status reports from each person to ensure that the assignments are being completed.

After you follow up on action items, you then inform attendees of progress made since the meeting ended. This can be done by collating the information you've gathered about the action items and then creating a progress report that you can e-mail to attendees.

Question

What are the responsibilities of a leader in relation to closing and following up a meeting?

Options:

1. Close the meeting before discussing parked items 2. Check to see if action items are being completed 3. Circulate the meeting record to attendees
4. Include details of the next meeting in the minutes 5. Provide attendees with progress reports
6. Ask attendees to summarize the meeting accomplishments in their own time Answer

Option 1: *This option is incorrect. A meeting should be closed when all the agenda items have been discussed, unless participants have agreed to discuss parked items at a later meeting.*

Option 2: *This option is correct. Checking what progress has been made in relation to action items is a responsibility of following up a meeting.*

Option 3: *This option is correct. Meeting leaders should circulate the meeting record to attendees as part of their responsibilities in following up a meeting.*

Option 4: *This option is correct. The time and date of the next meeting should be included in the minutes of the meeting.*

Option 5: *This option is correct. One of the responsibilities of a meeting leader when following up a meeting is to provide attendees with progress reports.*

Option 6: *This option is incorrect. When closing a meeting, a meeting leader should summarize accomplishments and make attendees aware of the next steps.*

Summary

When you close a meeting, you want to send participants away with a positive feeling that reflects their satisfaction with what they've accomplished in the meeting. You should close a meeting when you reach the end of the agenda or when you run out of time.

To follow up on a meeting you should send the minutes of the meeting to participants, follow up on actions taken, and inform attendees of progress made.

DEALING WITH COMMON MEETING PROBLEMS

How do you feel about business meetings? Do you dread attending because you think they're dull, unproductive, and disorganized? Or do you look forward to the chance to coordinate efforts, collaborate on issues, garner support for ideas, solve problems, and make consensus-based decisions?

How you feel about meetings will likely depend on your own experience – whether meetings you've attended were effective and efficient, or whether they were unfocused and out of control. But good meetings don't just happen. It takes a conscientious and ongoing effort to make meetings productive, worthwhile, and satisfying.

As a meeting leader, understanding the characteristics of effective business meetings will help you take positive, collaborative steps to address issues and make your own meetings more efficient, productive, timely, and enjoyable.

This course deals with appropriate ways to address common problems of business meetings. You'll learn about the value of conducting effective meetings and about practices to evaluate effectiveness. You'll discover how to intervene appropriately to address problems that occur during meetings, including issues of decorum and productivity problems. And you'll learn about how to handle the special challenges of virtual meetings.

INTERVENING TO IMPROVE MEETING EFFECTIVENESS

Evaluating effectiveness of a meeting

Put simply, a meeting is a gathering of two or more people to collectively accomplish what those individuals cannot do alone. In business, meetings are an integral part of corporate culture. When business meetings are conducted and led effectively, they can contribute significantly to the success and growth of an organization.

Consider Michelle, a manager at a financial services company. She understands meetings are important, and holds monthly staff meetings for her department. She has just completed one of those meetings. Although scheduled for an hour, the meeting lasted closer to two. But despite the excess time, Michelle is concerned that her team hasn't achieved anything concrete.

Many meeting leaders face concerns similar to Michelle's.

What these leaders need is a way to evaluate the effectiveness of their meetings.

Question

As a meeting leader, why do you think it's important to evaluate the effectiveness of your meetings?

Options:

1. It reinforces positive behavior
2. It shows group members how to improve their participation
3. It reveals ways to adjust planning and facilitation to improve

future meetings
4. It shows group members that you value their time and participation
5. It will make your meetings shorter
6. It will mean less work for you

Answer

Option 1: This option is correct. Evaluating meetings brings forth issues that can be corrected
to improve behavior.

Option 2: This option is correct. By identifying effective and ineffective behavior, you'll show group members - and yourself - how to be more productive.

Option 3: This option is correct. Evaluation reveals the time and effort spent on different aspects of a meeting. This allows you to adjust planning and facilitation to improve future meetings.

Option 4: This option is correct. By taking the time to evaluate a meeting, you show your team members that their participation is both valued and expected.

Option 5: This option is incorrect. Your meetings won't necessarily be shorter, but they will be more productive and efficient.

Option 6: This option is incorrect. Effective meetings won't mean less work for you, but they make the work you do more productive.

After the meeting, Michelle considers how it progressed. At the start, the team spent a lot of time discussing the previous meeting.

The team debated who had promised to do what and how much had actually been achieved. There were disagreements, although Michelle couldn't tell if issues were resolved because everyone was talking at once.

During the meeting there were several delays as employees left to get materials. And although the new computer system was the main subject of the meeting, only one IT employee attended and he had little to contribute to the discussion.

So how do you evaluate meeting effectiveness? By answering specific questions based on key criteria, and by engaging the other meeting participants in the process.

Answering specific questions based on key criteria is important to help you objectively analyze the effectiveness of your meetings.

The questions you ask will depend on the criteria of the meeting. You can tailor them to the purpose of your specific meeting.

There are many criteria that contribute to an effective meeting:
- location and venue of the meeting
- pace of the proceedings
- participation and collaboration of the participants
- focus on the meeting's objectives
- adherence to order and procedure
- conduct of the participants
- productivity of the meeting, and
- clarity of the next steps to take

See each type of criterion for examples of questions to ask yourself.

Location and venue
Was the location convenient to get to? Was the venue comfortable and free of distractions? Did all the equipment function?

Pace
Were there points where the meeting dragged? Was enough time allocated to agenda items?

Participation and collaboration
Was participation balanced and equitable? Did participants cooperate to achieve objectives?

Focus on objectives
Did discussion stay on point? Was the agenda respected?

Order and procedure
Were agreed-upon rules of order and procedure followed? Was a clear process followed for decision-making?

Conduct
Were participants civil and courteous? Was behavior respectful to others?

Productivity

Were objectives met? Was progress made clear to participants?

Clarity

Were action items for the next meeting clearly outlined? Does everyone know what they have to do next?

Engaging participants in evaluation

When you're evaluating your meeting, engaging other participants will give you multiple perspectives. Evaluation helps participants to assess their performance, both individually and collectively. It also helps them to become more aware of factors that detract from the effectiveness of meetings.

You can help engage other meeting participants in evaluating effectiveness by inviting their feedback, either before or after the meeting. Effective tools and techniques for eliciting feedback include focusing on positives first, recognizing good ideas publicly, and using evaluation forms.

Good meeting facilitators invite and welcome honest, specific feedback from participants because it helps them to improve the effectiveness and efficiency of future meetings.

A short assessment at the end of the meeting can garner valuable group feedback from participants. It helps to focus on the positives first, before you start discussing what needs to improve. Support participants to suggest things that the group should "keep on doing," or "encourage more of" in future meetings.

Motivation is important when you solicit feedback at meetings. Make sure that when someone offers an insightful observation or a good idea, you recognize it publicly, and show your appreciation for positive participation.

You may choose to get feedback from meeting participants after the meeting is over.

Sometimes participants are more open and honest in one-on-one conversations, or when they are doing written assessments.

An evaluation form is a useful tool for encouraging people to contribute to the feedback process. The information and data can be collated and the results can be discussed at the next scheduled meeting.

A typical evaluation form asks meeting participants to rate meeting criteria on a scale of one to ten, with one being poor and ten being excellent. It should also include space for participants to note feedback such as what worked well, what could be better, and ideas for improvement.

An evaluation form asks participants to rate eight criteria on a scale of one to ten. In order the criteria are: Location and venue, Pace of the meeting, Participation and collaboration, Focus on objectives, Adherence to order and procedure, Conduct of participants, Productivity, and Clarity of next steps.

Question
What are some good practices for evaluating meeting effectiveness?
Options:
1. Ask questions based on essential criteria to assess the meeting
2. Take time at the end of the meeting to evaluate the proceedings
3. Request feedback after the meeting
4. Use evaluation forms to solicit information and data
5. Recognize good ideas publicly
6. Start the assessment with issues that need improvement
7. Make sure all the participants give open feedback before the end of each meeting

Answer

Option 1: *This option is correct. Asking questions based on key criteria can provide specific and valuable information.*

Option 2: *This option is correct. Inviting feedback inside the meeting encourages group participation.*

Option 3: *This option is correct. Some participants are more open in one-on-one conversations, or written assessments requested after the meeting.*

Option 4: *This option is correct. Evaluation forms are a useful tool for rating meeting effectiveness and gathering feedback.*

Option 5: *This option is correct. It's important to encourage and sup-*

port participants by recognizing good ideas publicly, and focusing on positive feedback first.

Option 6: *This option is incorrect. It's important to start with positives first to garner valuable group feedback.*

Option 7: *This option is incorrect. Sometimes participants are more honest in one-on-one conversations after the meeting, or when they are doing written assessments.*

Intervening in a meeting

After your meeting has been evaluated, you may realize it wasn't as effective as it could have been and that you need to take steps to improve future meetings. Some common meeting problems can be eliminated through better planning, which includes clarifying the objectives and agenda for your meetings, setting ground rules, planning appropriate meeting processes, and double-checking your venue and equipment.

Good preparation can circumvent many meeting problems. But sometimes issues arise within an ongoing meeting that can derail even the best-laid plans. These types of issues arise largely from human factors.

Reflect

In your experience, what kinds of issues would warrant the use of intervention from a leader during a meeting?

You may have noted that a meeting leader could use intervention to diffuse conflicts, or to encourage participation in the meeting. Or you may have said that intervention can be used to guide and refocus behaviors such as dominance, rambling, distraction, or emotional outbursts.

However you decide to use intervention, keep in mind its main purpose is to keep the meeting on track, while making sure the needs of the participants are met.

Issues requiring intervention during ongoing meetings generally fall into three categories: a lack of order and decorum, poor productivity, and unbalanced participation.

There are three basic steps to follow when preparing to intervene in a meeting. First, observe and note the type of behavior. Next, infer the meaning and motivation underlying the behavior. Then decide how and when to intervene if the behavior is impairing the progress of the meeting.

Anwar is leading a project team meeting at an architectural firm. His assistant manager, Tracy, is currently summarizing the recent changes to the project requested by the client. Anwar observes that Tracy has begun repeating herself.

Anwar notices that Tracy seems nervous and infers that she has lost her focus and begun to ramble. Anwar decides to wait for a pause and then intervene to get the meeting back on track.

Once you determine an intervention is necessary, you should follow four core guidelines of intervention. Remember that your purpose is not to reprimand participants, but to steer them back toward behavior that fits with the meeting's agreed-upon rules of order and procedure. The intervention guidelines are to try nonverbal interventions first, communicate your intent, be positive, and collaborate on a solution.

See each meeting intervention guideline for more information.

Try nonverbal interventions first

A nonverbal intervention may be enough to get your meeting back on track. Examples include
making eye contact, raising your hand, pointing at participants to indicate turns to speak, or raising a finger to your lips to indicate silence. If nonverbal intervention doesn't work, you can move on to a verbal intervention.

Communicate your intent

The context of your intervention is important. Whenever possible, state your intent and reason for the intervention. For example if a participant is dominating the conversation, you might say "I'm going to ask you to leave it there. We have just enough time to invite the other participants to react to your proposal." It may help to refer to the rules of order for the meeting. For example, "Each person has five minutes to speak, so I'm going to ask the other participants to give their opinions now."

Be positive

Many forms of disruptive behavior come from a positive source. For example, enthusiasm or passion for a subject can cause people to interrupt other participants or to veer off-topic toward their own interests. Or a speaker may ramble or lose focus because they're nervous.

When you intervene, you should do so with a positive attitude. Use affirmative phrasing and avoid reprimands. It also helps to phrase your intervention constructively, stating what it is you want the participants to do. For example you would say "Sandra, you're good at analysis, I'd like to hear your opinion" rather than "Sandra, you haven't made much of a contribution."

Collaborate on a solution

Remember that when you're in a meeting, you're part of a collaborative group. So it's important to be inclusive, not autocratic when you're intervening. Techniques include ending the intervention with a question, and requesting the support and input of the group. Using inclusive language such as "we" instead of "I" promotes inclusion and teamwork.

For example, what if two members of the group are talking together and not paying attention? An effective intervention statement might be "Julia and Sanjay, we're reviewing the proposal right now. If we need to, we can have a short discussion when we're done. Is that OK with everyone?"

Question

You're leading an interdepartmental meeting to review budgeting decisions for the next fiscal year. Each manager has been allotted 10 minutes, but Olivia, the marketing manager, has been speaking for close to 15 minutes.

What would be an appropriate first response?

Options:

1. Let her finish speaking and reprimand her after the meeting
2. Interrupt her and remind her the time is up
3. Make eye contact and raise your hand

Answer

EFFECTIVE BUSINESS MEETINGS

Option 1: *This option is incorrect. Your first step shouldn't be to reprimand meeting participants, but to encourage participation according to the agreed-upon rules of order.*
Option 2: *This option is incorrect. The best way to begin an intervention is to try nonverbal signals such as eye contact.*
Option 3: *This is the correct option. Nonverbal signals are a good first step in intervention. Often this is all it takes to get the participant back on track.*

A simple nonverbal intervention can be very effective in getting participants to refocus on meeting objectives. But sometimes it takes more than that.
For serious or persistent issues, you may want to talk to meeting participants privately before or after the meeting.
For example, if Jim has a tendency to interrupt, you could mention it to him after the meeting, citing examples. Then, before the next meeting, gently remind him that everyone is to speak in turn.

Question
Remember Olivia? You're still at the meeting and you've used a nonverbal signal to indicate she's over her time limit. However, Olivia is still going on about her department's budget.
What is the best example of an effective intervention statement?
Options:
1. "We've heard the main points of your presentation, Olivia. Does anyone have any questions before we move on?"
2. "Olivia, forgive me for interrupting but we're running over our time. If everyone agrees, I'd like us to move on to the sales manager's report. Is that acceptable to everyone?"
3. "All right, Olivia. I think that's enough for now. I need to make sure there's time for the sales manager's report."

Answer
Option 1: *This option is incorrect. You were inclusive, and you ended*

with a question. However, you didn't communicate your intent or rationale for intervening.

Option 2: *This is the correct option. A good intervention statement communicates your intent, is positive, and collaborates on a solution. Also, finishing with a question shows inclusion.*

Option 3: *This option is incorrect. You communicated your intent, but you weren't very positive. And using "I" instead of "we" isn't collaborative.*

Summary

Evaluating the effectiveness of your meetings has many benefits. It can improve participation, reinforce positive behavior, help you demonstrate appreciation for group members, and improve the efficiency of future meetings. You can assess meeting effectiveness by asking questions based on key criteria, and by involving other participants.

If issues impairing effectiveness arise during a meeting, you'll need to intervene. These issues include a lack of order and decorum, poor productivity and momentum, and unbalanced participation. Try nonverbal interventions first. If you need to intervene, use a statement that communicates your intent, is positive, and collaborates on a solution.

HANDLING DECORUM AND PRODUCTIVITY PROBLEMS IN MEETINGS

Decorum and productivity
Conflict at meetings is inevitable. In fact it's to be expected when you deal with people with different values, backgrounds, and perspectives. When managed well, conflict can stimulate interest, innovation, and enthusiasm. But when managed poorly, it can lead to miscommunication, disengagement, and disrespect.
At any business meeting, it's the responsibility of the meeting leader to preserve order and decorum, and to keep the momentum focused on productivity.
No matter how well you've prepared, things can still go wrong in meetings. An effective leader needs to know how to encourage and facilitate productive discussion, interpret and apply the rules of order, and preserve decorum by handling disruptive behavior.

Issues of order and decorum
Meeting participants don't always behave in an orderly, respectful way, and sometimes maintaining order and decorum is a challenge. Violations of order and decorum include interruptions, side conversations, disputes, and personal attacks.
See each type of violation for more information.

Interruptions

Interruptions to meetings include participants speaking out of turn, cutting other people off, hijacking the conversation, or speaking over another person.

Side conversations

Side conversations are surreptitious communications that take place at the same time as someone else who's speaking. These include commenting to another person, whispering together, and passing notes.

Disputes

Disputes are conflicts between participants or between a participant and the meeting leader.

These include arguments, power struggles, quarrels, protestations, and emotional outbursts.

Personal attacks

Personal attacks are references to perceived negative characteristics of another person. Tactics include insulting or belittling the person. Attacks on a speaker include heckling – making disparaging comments to make the speaker appear foolish or less trustworthy.

As a meeting leader, your role is to help provide a safe environment where conflict can be put to use as a positive force. When you learn to recognize and handle problem behaviors, violations of order and decorum can be resolved or mitigated with effective intervention techniques.

Interruptions to the proceedings can throw a meeting off-track, and waste valuable time. Sometimes interruptions involve the whole group, and at other times you may be dealing with one challenging individual.

Whichever issue you're dealing with, you'll need to take action to help the group move forward.

To be an effective leader you need to be able to control a meeting quickly and tactfully. For example, if someone is interjecting or cutting off the speaker, ask the disruptive participant to wait for a turn, and assure everyone they'll have an opportunity. If everyone is talking at once, or too many people are vying for attention, establish a speaking lineup. For example you could say, "We'll go around the table taking turns to speak. Let's start with Anthony."

Side conversations are at best distracting, and at worst disrespectful and rude. In these situations, you'll need to stop the behavior.

Try a nonverbal signal, such as holding up your hand for quiet, or making eye contact and shaking your head to indicate the behavior is distracting.

If you're currently speaking, you could try pausing until the conversationalists notice that others are waiting for them to stop talking.

If a number of people are talking at once, or aren't paying attention, nonverbal signals may not work. In this case, you'll need to verbally indicate that the behavior should stop.

It can help to tactfully interject and ask if there's a problem. Remember to be sincere – embarrassing the conversationalists will just alienate them.

For example, you could say, "Suni and Bob, is there a problem? Was there something you didn't understand about what Xiao was saying?"

Sometimes, side conversations are meant to pull focus away from a speaker or a subject.

You should make sure you don't shift the attention of the group to the conversationalists by giving them the floor.

Instead of saying "Is there something you two want to share with the group?" you could say something like "Ida and Katherine, do you need some time to comment when Jai is finished his turn?"

Question
Match each circumstance to the most appropriate response for handling it during a meeting.
Options:
A. One participant cuts another off
B. Participants all seem to be talking at once

C. Two participants are talking to each other instead of listening
D. One participant is passing notes to another

Targets:
1. You could say, "Please raise your hand if you want to speak, Jan. Everyone will have an opportunity to be heard in turn."
2. You could say, "Can I have everyone's attention? Let's take turns to speak. Everyone will have two minutes, and we'll start with Tom."
3. Hold up your hand for silence and make eye contact with the disruptive participants.
4. You could say, "Declan, is there an issue you need clarified about what the speaker was saying?"

Answer

Participants who interrupt should be reminded of proper procedure, and reassured they'll have an opportunity to contribute.

If everyone is talking at once, establish a speaking lineup and give each person time to speak. Nonverbal signals can draw the attention of side conversationalists back to the meeting leader.

You can deal with side conversations by asking the talkers if there is a problem, then moving on with the meeting.

To succeed in business, people need to be able to persuade others to listen to their ideas, opinions, and ambitions. When objectives conflict, **disputes** can arise. In an effective meeting, conflict is a problem-solving process, not a competition.

In an effective meeting, group members feel free to consider all sides of an issue without fear of reprisal or derision.

But people can be emotionally attached to issues. When these emotions get out of hand, arguments and other disputes can disrupt proceedings.

It's essential you deal with unproductive conflict early, before it spirals out of control.

If a dispute is off topic, restate the objective being discussed and ask disruptive participants to move on. If the dispute is on topic, call attention to the objective and summarize the main points of both sides of the discussion. Then ask the larger group for input. For example, "Our objective is to schedule the new project. Zareen, you think we can be finished by June. Steve, you say August is more realistic. Let's hear from the rest of the group."

When you're dealing with a dispute, don't choose one side over another. As a meeting leader, your job is to remain neutral and persuade others to cooperate on reaching mutually agreeable solutions.

Reflect

What do you think could be done as a last resort when meeting disputes get out of control?

Dealing with disputes

You may have noted that stopping the meeting and taking a break can be an effective technique for coping with out-of-control disputes. Often, a short break will give participants time to cool down and get control of their emotions.

Sometimes disputes can escalate into **personal attacks**. Personal attacks can be a result of someone losing his temper. Or someone may think it's humorous to heckle a colleague. Still other people use personal attacks to intimidate, bully, and stifle others. Whatever the motivation, this type of behavior shouldn't be tolerated in a meeting. You need to be able to regain control of the meeting without widening the rift started by the disruptive participant.

A good technique is to state the behavior expected of participants by the group.

For example, the rules of order may state that participants are respectful when someone else is speaking, or that in a debate any disagreements are addressed to the meeting leader.

Remind participants to focus on the issue, and to avoid personal speculation or attacks.

A good technique to deal with personal attacks is to acknowledge proper meeting procedure and state the behavior expected of participants.

It can help to acknowledge that feelings aren't wrong, but expressing them in hurtful or inflammatory ways isn't part of proper meeting procedure.

Phrase your statements in terms of rules of order, not as a reprimand. For example, "Walter, we understand you feel strongly about the issue, but please confine your remarks to the agenda item."

You may also have to deal with disrespect. If Walter rolls his eyes or makes a face while another person is speaking, ask the speaker to pause.

Then address the group with a comment such as "Our rules are that we show respect when we listen to one another. May I assume we have the group's support?"

Question

Match each circumstance to the most appropriate response for handling it.

Options:
1. Two participants have opposing viewpoints on resolving an agenda item and the discussion is getting heated
2. Two participants are arguing about whether to turn up the heat in the room
3. A participant heckles a colleague during a presentation

Targets:
1. "Len thinks the solution is to increase the budget, but Hanna believes we need to extend the timeline. Let's get some ideas from the rest of the group."
2. "This discussion isn't relevant to our objective. Let's move on."
3. "Please focus on the issue and address any comments to the meeting leader as per our rules of order."

Answer

If a dispute is on topic, such as a debate about an agenda item, summarize each side, and ask the rest of the group for input.

If a dispute is off topic, such as a discussion about room temperature, then ask participants to move on.

If a participant is making personal remarks, such as heckling, insist that the focus remains on the issue and refer the person to the rules of order for the meeting.

Productivity issues

Even if everyone behaves with decorum, your meeting may not be productive. As a leader, you need to keep the meeting focused on productivity – achieving the objectives laid out in the agenda and managing the pace so participants' interest and commitment remain high.

Productivity suffers when meetings lose momentum, and participants disconnect from the process. Productivity issues include deadlock, loss of focus, and rambling.

See each productivity issue for more information.

Deadlock

Sometimes meetings stall because of deadlock – when no one has anything new to say but the team is unable to come to a decision or move on. Deadlock can be due to conflict, but is just as often a result of indecision or fear of making mistakes.

Loss of focus

Meetings can lose momentum when productive discussions lose focus and devolve into unfocused and off-topic group discussions.

Rambling

Rambling participants often have relevant opinions, but are unable to get their points across efficiently. They digress into other subjects, or repeatedly express the same points in different ways. They may use stories or scenarios to illustrate what they are saying, rather than stating a point.

When you're faced with deadlock, try a creative approach to create momentum. Use a "what if" question to spark debate, or ask participants with opposing viewpoints to list points they agree on. Sometimes all that's needed to re-energize the meeting is to take a short break. Or you could try moving on to the next agenda item, and then coming back to the deadlocked discussion.

Question

You're leading a meeting and the team is deadlocked.
What are appropriate responses to the situation?
Options:
1. "If no one is going to contribute to the discussion, I'll have to make the decision myself."
2. "We're going to get this done if we're here all day."
3. "Let's look at this another way. Francis, which of Jim's points do you agree with, and why?"
4. "All right everyone. Let's take a short break."

Answer

Option 1: This option is incorrect. To deal with deadlock you need to re-energize participants. You could try a creative approach to problem solving, or take a short break and then regroup.

Option 2: This option is incorrect. Meetings become deadlocked because people can't or won't make decisions. Just waiting around won't help.

Option 3: This option is correct. Creative approaches can help to change people's perspectives and stimulate debate.

Option 4: This option is correct. Sometimes taking a short break will help to re-energize the meeting.

It's not uncommon for conversations to drift off-topic during a meeting. To keep from losing focus, summarize progress and refer to the agenda as you deal with objectives.

For example, "We've covered the project timeline, so let's move on to the budget."

Consider using visual aids to track meeting progress. This adds interest and helps keep participants focused.

If you realize the focus of a meeting has drifted, use a casual but clear intervention. Firmly ask the group to get back on track. For example, "We've drifted off topic. Let's refocus on the budget."

If participants are reluctant to let go of the off-topic conversation, refer the issue to "other business" – sometimes called the "parking lot."

This is an item at the end of the agenda where participants can discuss unscheduled topics.

Rambling is another issue that can deaden the pace of a meeting. Rambling happens for various reasons. Some speakers ramble because they're nervous or shy. Others enjoy the attention of having their say or may be used to a different style of meeting.

Your first tactic in dealing with a rambler should be to use a nonverbal signal. Look the person in the eyes, and raise your hand to indicate a pause. If you're familiar with the rambling participant, you could use humor by signaling "move along" or "wrap it up."

Then try verbal intervention, asking the rambler to sum things up. Be polite so you don't embarrass the speaker. For example, "Jason, we need to move on to other issues. Is everyone clear on the points Jason was making?" Or "Maya, if you had to sum up your main point in one sentence, what would it be?"

Michelle is a manager at a financial services company. She is currently leading a staff meeting with her team. Antonio is giving the team a project update. However, he has been speaking for a while, and has begun to repeat his points.

Follow along as Michelle deals with Antonio's rambling and her team's loss of focus.

Antonio: And as I was saying, the market forces and the general spheres of influence we're dealing with have slightly impacted our ability to adjust to our business performance indicator metrics.

Michelle: (Raises her hand) *Michelle raises her hand.*

Antonio: Though our productivity levels are under siege from varied psychodemographic forces, our capacity for resilience has resulted only in a minor bottleneck.

Michelle: Thanks, Antonio. We have to move on, so would you summarize your point in one sentence for the group? *Michelle says, pleasantly.*

Antonio: The project is running a day late.

Pippa: That always seems to happen. You never hear about projects running early.

Lee: My last project ran early, at least for a while.

Pippa: Was that the one you worked on with Norm? He sits near

me and he was always complaining about it.
Pippa says, gossiping.
Lee: What was he saying? Was it anything about me?
Michelle: All right, everybody. Let's get back to business. We've finished with Antonio's update. The next item on the agenda is reviewing expense reports. Lee, you're up first.
Michelle says, pleasantly.
Michelle correctly handled the issues of rambling and loss of focus in her meeting.

When Antonio went on too long and began to repeat himself, Michelle tried a nonverbal signal to indicate he should pause. When Antonio didn't pick up his cue, Michelle interjected. She noted that it was time to move on and asked Antonio to sum up his point.

When the group lost focus and began to drift into a personal conversation about another project, Michelle summarized the progress, and asked the group to get back on track with the agenda.

Question

You're a manager at a marketing company and you're meeting with your team to do some strategic planning for a client. Your assistant, Felix, is describing the ideal target market, but instead of summarizing, he has decided to read his entire 12-page report. What are the best responses to deal with Felix?

Options:
1. Signal Felix to wrap up his presentation.
2. Interrupt Felix and tell him the other participants can read his report if they want all the details. Then remind him not to be so verbose in the future.
3. Let Felix finish reading his report.
4. Remind Felix that team members have a copy of his report and that time is limited. Then ask him if he would quickly summarize his main points before the meeting moves to the next agenda item.

Answer

Option 1: *This option is correct. A nonverbal signal may be what the*

rambling participant needs to encourage him to finish speaking.
Option 2: This option is incorrect. Your intervention should be helpful and polite, so you don't embarrass or alienate the speaker.
Option 3: This option is incorrect. As meeting leader, it's your responsibility to maintain the pace and momentum of the meeting.
Option 4: This option is correct. A good approach is to indicate it's time to move on, and then politely ask the rambling participant to briefly sum up his message.

Over time, you'll develop the skill of estimating how much time you'll need for your meeting, and for each agenda item.
But when meeting discussions are productive and constructive, it may be necessary to extend their allotted time.
If you need to exceed the planned time for an agenda item, a speaker, or the meeting itself, seek approval from the group. Make sure you have agreement for the extension.

Question
Your meeting at the marketing company is about halfway through. During a discussion about advertising media, the group has drifted into a conversation about favorite television shows.
Which are the most appropriate responses to refocus the group on the meeting objectives?
Options:
1. "That's enough off-topic discussion. I don't want to have to tell you again."
2. "Well, I guess it's time for a break. We'll can talk about our favorite shows over some refreshments. Who's buying?"
3. "All right everyone. You can see from the flip chart we've covered the first four agenda items. Let's finish the media discussion, and then cover new business and we're done."
4. "This is interesting, but not relevant to the task at hand. Let's get back to the

Answer

Option 1: This option is incorrect. You should intervene when the group loses focus, but you should be polite as well as firm.

Option 2: This option is incorrect. A deadlocked team might need a break, but when a team is wandering off-topic you really need to intervene to get it back on track.

Option 3: This option is correct. Summarizing the progress the group members have made can help get them back on track when they lose focus. As well, visual aids can help keep the group's attention.

Option 4: This option is correct. When the group wanders off-topic, you should firmly but politely intervene to get the meeting back on course.

Summary

It's a meeting leader's responsibility to preserve order and decorum, and to keep the momentum focused on productivity. Violations of order and decorum include interruptions, side conversations, disputes, and personal attacks. Productivity issues include loss of group focus, deadlock, and rambling participants.

IMPROVING PARTICIPATION IN MEETINGS

Meeting participation

Managing participation means shaping a meeting so that each participant has the opportunity to comment on topics, express opinions, and work to influence decisions. However, each individual member of the group will have different communication and participation styles. For example, there will be some participants who are happy to do all the talking, and others whose tendency is to sit back and say little.

If participation isn't managed effectively, then assertive, outspoken, and confident group members may tend to dominate the proceedings. Submissive, less confident, or inexperienced group members may remain quiet. Without balanced and diverse input into a meeting, there's a real danger that the quality of decisions will suffer.

As a meeting leader, your role in promoting and balancing participation is that of a facilitator. You can't just hope that participation will happen. Nor can you demand it. During a meeting, the leader has two main jobs: to draw out quiet participants and to prevent dominant participants from monopolizing the discussion.

A good facilitator manages the flow of the discussion and stays focused on accomplishing the objectives of the meeting.

It's also important to be sensitive to the motivations of your meeting participants. It's vital to respect individual differences and proceed carefully to help people optimize their contributions.

Unbalanced participation can lead to a number of issues that can affect the quality of a meeting. These include a patronizing or intimidating atmosphere, overparticipation in the proceedings, and uncommunicative group members.

See each unbalanced participation issue for more information.

Intimidating atmosphere

In a meeting with a patronizing or intimidating atmosphere, assertive participants prioritize their own agendas, while more passive group members push back by passively refusing to participate. This can result when more aggressive participants use bullying or other intimidation tactics to get their own way.

Overparticipation

Most meetings will have at least one participant who isn't afraid to speak up and give an opinion. But sometimes a person's overparticipation in the proceedings can dominate a meeting.

This isn't necessarily due to any malice. Some people are very enthusiastic or passionate. Others may have a lot of experience and become a "resident expert" on certain subjects. Others just like to hear themselves speak.

Uncommunicative members

People have a variety of reasons for not contributing to discussions. They may be shy, or intimidated, or want to avoid conflict. They may feel unworthy to give an opinion because they're young or inexperienced. Or they may feel apathetic toward meetings because of bad experiences in the past.

To circumvent a patronizing or **intimidating atmosphere** in a meeting, make sure to set a welcoming tone right from the beginning. And be prepared to give extra support to first-time or reluctant speakers.

To maintain an open and welcoming atmosphere, make it clear from the outset that everyone will be asked to contribute to the meeting. For example, "There are a lot of diverse perspectives in the room and we want to hear from everyone."

Don't let strong-willed participants intimidate quieter group members. If you notice that a first-time speaker seems eager to say something, give the person the opportunity to make her point without interruption. You could say "It's time for Iman to give her opinion on the issue."

If a shy participant's ideas are challenged by others in the group, support the participant by pointing out the positive aspects of his ideas. For example, "Tony raised a legitimate concern that warrants more discussion."

Overparticipation in the proceedings is a tricky meeting issue to handle. You should control dominant participants' behavior, but without dampening their enthusiasm or commitment. You'll need to intervene only if dominant participants' behavior is shutting out other group members. You might consider using a speakers' lineup, or setting a rule that no one speaks a second time until everyone has had the chance to speak a first time.

If a participant persists in dominating conversation, you may have to interrupt tactfully, and invite a first-time speaker to contribute.

For example, you could say, "Mark, I appreciate your enthusiasm, but I'm going to ask you to wait because you've already had a chance to comment. We haven't heard from anyone in the Finance Department yet. Trevor, did you have a point you wanted to raise?"

If you're aware that certain people tend to overparticipate, you could speak to them privately - before the meeting or on a break - and encourage them to give others a chance to contribute.

Uncommunicative members of a group may just need encouragement. You may want to ask them directly to participate, but don't put them on the spot if they don't seem ready.

Look for nonverbal cues that the person wants to make a contribution. When someone leans forward, seems to have a quizzical expression, or moves his head in agreement or disagreement, you may ask something like, "Felix, it looks like you have something to say about this topic. We'd love to hear your thoughts about it."

One way to ensure that speakers are ready to contribute is to use a group technique to elicit discussion. For example, you could use a speakers' lineup or a round-robin technique, where everyone comments or offer ideas in turn before the topic is debated.

Question
What techniques will encourage balanced participation in a meeting?
Options:
1. State that you would like to hear from all participants
2. Make sure first-time speakers have the chance to give their opinions without interruption
3. Speak to potentially dominant meeting participants before the meeting
4. Use a round-robin technique or a speakers' lineup
5. Support a point made by a shy participant
6. Make sure subject experts always speak first in a conversation
7. Let each participant finish speaking before you move to the next

Answer
Option 1: *This option is correct. Setting a welcoming tone helps participants feel comfortable and encouraged to speak.*
Option 2: *This option is correct. Supporting first-time speakers shows you encourage their full participation.*
Option 3: *This option is correct. Speaking to a dominant speaker privately can circumvent a potential issue of overparticipation.*
Option 4: *This option is correct. Using a group technique such as a round-robin or establishing a speakers' lineup ensures everyone has a turn to speak.*
Option 5: *This option is correct. Supporting the points of reluctant or shy participants is one way to encourage them to contribute.*
Option 6: *This option is incorrect. Giving special consideration to certain group members can intimidate less-experienced participants.*

Option 7: *This option is incorrect. Some group members may tend to overparticipate and shut out less-dominant group members. You should intervene to make sure participation is balanced.*

Michelle is a manager at a financial services company. She's currently in a budget meeting with her team. The team is discussing an agenda item.

Follow along as Michelle deals with balancing participation in a meeting.

Michelle: Thanks very much, Antonio. Your suggestions for the training budget were insightful. And detailed. Is there anyone else who would like to comment?

Michelle says, pleasantly.

Antonio: Actually, I have a few more points. I just found the rest of my notes. So anyway, I was talking about how I think we can optimize the training budget.

Antonio says, enthusiastically.

Michelle: Antonio, I know you're keen on this subject, but I'm going to ask you wait until everyone else has had their turn to comment.

Michelle says, pleasantly.

Michelle: So let's finish the round-robin. Pippa, Antonio, and Lee have all spoken. Sven, it's your turn. Do you have any ideas or suggestions?

Michelle says, pleasantly.

Sven: Well, it's not my area of expertise. But...oh never mind. *Sven says, shyly.*

Michelle: We'd like to hear what you have to say. Everyone's input is important.

Michelle says, pleasantly.

Sven: OK then. I do have a few ideas. *Sven says, happily.*

Michelle correctly dealt with balancing participation at a meeting. She tactfully intervened when Antonio was overparticipating, and she used a round-robin technique to ensure balanced participation. This allowed her to draw out Sven, who had been uncommunicative to that point in the discussion.

Question

You're a project manager at an architectural firm. You're leading a meeting to plan the schedule for a new project to build an office tower. June is your accountant. She has been speaking at length on the need to control costs. Neil is the production manager. He has started to speak a few times, but hasn't been able to make a point. You determine you'll need to intervene to manage balanced participation at the meeting.

Match each meeting participant with examples of intervention statements to the appropriate meeting participant. Each participant may match to more than one statement.

Options:

A. June B. Neil

Targets:

1. "We understand what you're saying. We're going to move on now so everyone has a turn."
2. "Would you share your opinion with the group?"
3. "I sense you have something to say. did you have a point you wanted to raise?"
4. "Meeting rules are that everybody has a chance to speak. If the group agrees, we'll come back to you after that if there's time."

Answer

June is dominating the proceedings. This means you need to tactfully intervene and remind her to let other participants speak.

Neil is uncommunicative. He'll be encouraged to speak if you give him an opportunity to make his point.

Neil seems intimidated. He'll be more likely to participate if you're welcoming and supportive of him.

June is overparticipating in the meeting. You need to remind her of meeting rules about participation. It can also help to draw support from the group.

Intervening appropriately

EFFECTIVE BUSINESS MEETINGS

In an ideal world, meetings would consist of topical, orderly discussions leading logically to effective decisions. But in the real world, keeping a meeting organized, inclusive, and moving forward is an ongoing task. As a meeting leader, you'll need to be on the lookout for many types of decorum, productivity, and participation problems that could arise.

Case Study: Question 1 of 3
Scenario
For your convenience, the case study is repeated with each question.
You're an editorial manager at a publishing house. Your team is meeting to decide which books will be included in the spring lineup.

Question
What is the major problem facing this meeting group?
Options:
1. Unbalanced participation
2. Lack of productivity
3. Violations of order and decorum
Answer
Option 1: *This option is incorrect. The main characteristics of unbalanced participation are a*
patronizing or intimidating atmosphere, overparticipation by some members, and a lack of communication from others.
Option 2: *This option is incorrect. The main characteristics of a meeting suffering from lack of productivity are deadlock, loss of focus, and rambling participants.*
Option 3: *This is the correct option. The interruptions, side conversations, disputes, and personal attacks mark this as a meeting suffering from violations of order and decorum.*

Case Study: Question 2 of 3
Scenario
For your convenience, the case study is repeated with each question.
You're an editorial manager at a publishing house. Your team is meeting to decide which books will be included in the spring

lineup.

Question

You've asked the group members to recommend three fiction titles to feature in the spring catalog. Len, one of the copywriters, raises his hand to speak, but is interrupted by Nancy, a junior editor. She questions his expertise to comment and proposes the subject be "left to the experts."

What is the best example of an intervention statement to deal with this issue?

Options:
1. "Pardon me, Nancy. Len, go ahead. I'd like to hear what you have to say."
2. "Nancy, let me just stop you. Our rules of order allow each person to speak in turn without interruption. After Len has spoken, can we hear from others on this issue?"
3. "Nancy, stop that. It's rude. According to our rules, Len has a right to speak even if he's just a copywriter. Remember that everyone in the group agreed to follow the rules of order."

Answer

Option 1: This option is incorrect. This intervention statement politely stopped Nancy's interruption but didn't communicate your intent to encourage inclusive participation. Also, the use of "I" wasn't very collaborative.

Option 2: This is the correct option. This is a tactful intervention statement that communicates your intent, and it's positive and inclusive in tone.

Option 3: This option is incorrect. This intervention statement stopped Nancy's interruption, but it wasn't positive in tone.

Case Study: Question 3 of 3

Scenario

For your convenience, the case study is repeated with each question.

You're an editorial manager at a publishing house. Your team is meeting to decide which books will be included in the spring lineup.

Question

What example statements would be the most appropriate for improving the issues that plague this meeting?

Options:
1. "Remember to raise your hands if you wish to speak."
2. "Would the junior editors cease their conversation, please? The rules allow one person to speak at a time."
3. "Our objective is to choose one non-fiction title for spring. Angie wants the cookbook. William wants the self-help book. Will the rest of the group please comment?"
4. "Tami, we understand you feel strongly, but please confine your remarks to the topic and not the speaker."
5. "In the interests of time, I'm going to make the decisions." 6. "We'll just sit and wait until everyone's finished talking."

Answer

Option 1: This option is correct. When interruptions are a problem, remind participants of rules of order for decorous behavior.

Option 2: This option is correct. Side conversations are distracting. One way to deal with them is to remind participants of the meeting rules for behavior.

Option 3: This option is correct. Deal with disputes by calling attention to the objective of the debate and summarizing the main points of both sides of the discussion. Then turn the debate over to the group.

Option 4: This option is correct. To deal with a personal attack, you need to regain control of the meeting without widening the rift started by the disruptive participant.

Option 5: This option is incorrect. Your job as meeting leader is to make sure the proceedings are inclusive.

Option 6: This option is incorrect. A meeting leader should make sure proceedings are organized, and moving forward.

Summary

Meeting leaders need to balance the participation of individuals, while maintaining a respect for group objectives. You can deal with a patronizing or intimidating atmosphere by setting a welcoming tone and supporting first-time speakers.

You can handle overparticipation by tactfully interrupting and inviting first-time speakers to contribute, establishing a speakers' lineup, or speaking privately to the overparticipator.

DEALING WITH THE CHALLENGES OF VIRTUAL MEETINGS

Virtual meetings and dispersed teams

Holding meetings in a single location is a long standing business tradition. But today, more and more people are working in dispersed teams – teams where the members are separated by time and distance. On dispersed teams, the team members aren't all located in the same building. In fact, they may not even be located in the same country. This means meetings need to be held with the use of communication technology. These "virtual meetings" bring a new set of challenges for meeting leaders.

The technology for virtual meetings may use only audio, known as audioconferencing. It may use audio and video, known as videoconferencing. Or it may be through computers enabled by the web, known as web conferencing.

Dispersed teams operate in an environment almost completely dependent on technology. For teams to thrive and flourish in a virtual setting, team leaders need to develop a new way of thinking about communication.

As a meeting leader, you'll use many of the same skills for planning and leading virtual meetings as you use for regular meetings. You'll need to ensure that meetings are effective, balanced, and productive, and that group members participate and work toward achieving objectives.

But in a virtual meeting you'll also have to manage differences in time, technology, and in cultural connections between team members.

The main issues that arise with virtual meetings are misunderstandings due to cultural differences, lost time or participation due to limitations of technology, inattention and loss of focus by group members, and communication issues and participation problems stemming from the use of technology.

See each issue for more information.

Cultural differences

Dispersed teams often include participants from different cultures, as well as different geographical locales. Understanding cultural differences is essential for a team to work together effectively. You should remind participants to avoid using colloquialisms, metaphors, jargon, slang, and culturally specific references and humor. This could also be added to the meeting's rules of order.

Keep communication differences in mind as well. For example, in some cultures silence means agreement, while in others it signals disagreement.

Limitations of technology

Meetings can be disrupted if the technology doesn't function well, or if participants don't know how to use it. Familiarize group members with how to use the communication technology, and make contingency plans for what to do if there are problems with transmission.

For example, if a videoconferencing technology isn't working, you may have to switch to an audioconference. In this case, you'd need to come up with new procedures for how to vote or how to get the attention of the meeting leader.

Inattention and loss of focus

It's not uncommon for meeting participants to become inattentive or to lose focus when they can't see each other. To keep them interested, use interactive and graphical elements to engage and focus participants' attention on the meeting.

For example, you could send them a printout or e-mail a slide show to help them follow along. Keep virtual meetings short, and ask participants for input on a regular basis.

Communication issues

It's easier to communicate in person than through technology. Misunderstandings can occur due to limitations of communication technology. When you're leading a virtual meeting, make sure everyone can be heard. Speak slowly and clearly and remind others to do so as well. Check frequently to make sure participants understand what's happening.

For example, in an audioconference it's often difficult to determine who is talking from voice alone. Ask participants to identify themselves by their name before they speak. This will also help you take notes or organize speakers' lineups.

Participation problems

Dispersed team members may not know each other as well as those on a regular team. They may be more reluctant to speak up or interrupt. Make sure to ask if there are questions and comments after every discussion. Use a speakers' lineup or round-robin to go around the "virtual room" and give participants a chance to speak.

If you're web conferencing you could add an instant messaging option. This allows participants to contact the meeting leader when they wish to speak or when they need clarification on a point.

Question
Match the virtual meeting problems to examples of actions that address them.

Options:
A. Participation problems
B. Inattention and loss of focus
C. Limitations of technology
D. Communication issues
E. Cultural differences

Targets:
      1. Use a round-robin technique to go around the virtual

room
2. Use interactive and graphical elements to engage participants in the meeting process
3. Create contingency plans for what to do if there are problems with the communication equipment
4. Speak slowly and clearly and make sure you can be heard by participants
5. Adopt a rule of order that the communication style of the meeting be free of slang, jargon, and cultural references

Answer

Round-robins and speakers' lineups are good techniques for encouraging participation in virtual meetings.

Interactive and graphical elements can help focus the attention of participants on the meeting.

If issues arise with the technology, it makes sense to have a backup plan to continue the meeting.

When you're using meeting technology, it's important to check that you and the other participants can all be heard.

Using socially or culturally specific language can cause misunderstanding and confusion with participants from outside the culture.

Facilitating virtual meetings

Virtual meetings have a lot of different elements that need to be tracked and monitored. You may find it useful to appoint someone as a meeting monitor. The monitor can track and update you on who is participating, whether the meeting is on schedule, how long people have been speaking, and, if you're using an instant messaging system, who requires clarification or has something to add. This frees you up to focus on the business at hand.

Voting is another important consideration in a virtual meeting. In a regular meeting, most decisions are made by verbal acknowledgment or a show of hands.

In a virtual meeting, you'll probably need to poll individual members one by one. You can do this verbally or with the use of an instant messenger.

EFFECTIVE BUSINESS MEETINGS

If the group is discussing sensitive or controversial information, you'll need to get assurance from participants that they are the only people privy to the discussion. In these cases, it may be preferable to ask members to send in their votes by fax, e-mail, or regular mail.

Question

Samir leads a dispersed team at a multinational energy company. His team has a short meeting by videoconference once a month. Samir leads the meetings. He makes sure to check frequently to make sure the participants understand what's going on and how the meeting is progressing. He frequently asks individual participants if they have any questions or contributions to make. Samir has also arranged for an instant messaging option so individuals can contact him if they want to speak, or if they need further clarification on an item.

Which common meeting problems will be addressed by Samir's efforts?

Options:

1. Cultural differences
2. Limitations of technology
3. Communication issues
4. Inattention and loss of focus 5. Participation problems

Answer

Option 1: *This option is incorrect. Samir didn't take any measures to prevent cultural differences from leading to misunderstanding.*

Option 2: *This option is incorrect. Samir didn't orient participants on how to use the technology, or present a contingency plan to use if the technology fails.*

Option 3: *This option is correct. Checking frequently to make sure participants understand what's going on helps with communication issues.*

Option 4: *This option is correct. Keeping virtual meetings short and calling on participants to contribute helps keep participants from losing attention and focus.*

Option 5: *This option is correct. Asking if there are questions or com-*

ments, and providing an instant messaging option to communicate with the meeting leader are both techniques for dealing with participation problems.

Summary

Virtual meetings bring together participants in different locations through the use of telecommunication applications. As a meeting leader, you need to take measures to mitigate common issues that arise with virtual meetings, including misunderstandings due to cultural differences, lost time or participation due to limitations of technology, inattention and loss of focus by group members, and communication issues and participation problems stemming from the use of technology.

Virtual meetings can be easier to lead when you appoint a meeting monitor to track participation, progress, and time.

www.ingramcontent.com/pod-product-compliance
Lightning Source LLC
Chambersburg PA
CBHW070416220526
45466CB00004B/1429